Strategic Talent Leadership for Educators

This book is designed to support the transformation of educators into strategic talent leaders. The author's research-based "Strategic Talent Leadership Framework" gives leaders the tools for acquiring, accelerating, advancing and assessing educator talent. Each chapter features an illustrative case, best practices, a ready-to-use tool for advancing those practices, a set of "talent analytics" and an action step planner. This guidebook is for education leaders who seek to assess current performance, adopt research-based strategies for engaging in strategic human capital practices, set goals around the use of those practices and measure the impact of their work on student outcomes. Accessible and actionable, *Strategic Talent Leadership for Educators* is not only a guide, but a toolkit for putting research into practice.

Amy A. Holcombe is a former public school teacher, principal, director of curriculum, director of Title I, magnet and specialized schools, and executive director of talent development for a large district. She is currently the Dean of the Stout School of Education at High Point University, USA.

Other Eye On Education Books Available from Routledge
(www.routledge.com/eyeoneducation)

Strategic Talent Leadership for Educators

A Practical Toolkit

Amy A. Holcombe

Routledge
Taylor & Francis Group

NEW YORK AND LONDON

First published 2021
by Routledge
52 Vanderbilt Avenue, New York, NY 10017

and by Routledge
2 Park Square, Milton Park, Abingdon, Oxon, OX14 4RN

Routledge is an imprint of the Taylor & Francis Group, an informa business

© 2021 Taylor & Francis

Library of Congress Cataloging-in-Publication Data
Names: Holcombe, Amy A., author.
Title: Strategic talent leadership for educators : a practical toolkit /
Amy A. Holcombe.
Identifiers: LCCN 2020008100 (print) | LCCN 2020008101 (ebook) | ISBN
9780367423209 (hardback) | ISBN 9780367425661 (paperback) | ISBN
9780367853501 (ebook)
Subjects: LCSH: Teachers--Rating of--Handbooks, manuals, etc. |
Teachers--In-service training--Handbooks, manuals, etc. | Teacher
effectiveness--Handbooks, manuals, etc. | Educational
leadership--Handbooks, manuals, etc. | Teacher-principal
relationships--Handbooks, manuals, etc.
Classification: LCC LB2838 .H537 2020 (print) | LCC LB2838 (ebook) | DDC
371.14/4--dc23
LC record available at https://lccn.loc.gov/2020008100
LC ebook record available at https://lccn.loc.gov/2020008101

ISBN: 978-0-367-42320-9 (hbk)
ISBN: 978-0-367-42566-1 (pbk)
ISBN: 978-0-367-85350-1 (ebk)

Typeset in Optima
by Cenveo® Publisher Services

TD...All Day!

Contents

Illustrations

Figures

Tables

Introduction

Becoming a strategic talent leader begins at the front door of your school—who you let in and who you let out. It is your talent gateway. Nationally, school districts allocate 80–85 percent of their budget toward personnel (National Center for Education Statistics, 2018). These dollars pay for the salaries and benefits of the principals, teachers and school support personnel charged with providing students a quality education. These teachers and principals drive 58 percent of the variance in student achievement (Hattie, 2011; RAND Education, 2012). Collectively, they have the largest impact on student academic outcomes compared to all other factors. When considered together, the personnel costs and academic impacts of teachers and principals make them the most strategic resource any school or school district can leverage to transform schools. The best school improvement plan is a strategic talent leadership plan.

In the past 50 years, there has been a shift in principal preparation and training away from preparing strong managers to preparing instructional leaders. But, principals don't lead instruction, they lead people. Teachers don't lead instruction; they lead student learning. They facilitate the process of students discovering, applying and retaining skills and knowledge. In order to do so effectively, they need leaders who know how to support them in facilitating the instruction that leads to learning. They need strategic talent leaders. And, strategic talent leaders need a toolkit.

In 2016, the Center for American progress surveyed schools across the nation to learn about their human capital practices. What they found were outdated, nonexistent practices and irrelevant approaches to working with modern job seekers (Konoske-Graf, Partelow, & Benner, 2016). In these and other school districts, educator talent leadership is being driven by human resource departments charged with hiring, providing health and wellness benefits, setting salary schedules and, in unfortunate cases, employee termination. Many times, principals' only interaction with a human resources department is when they need to fill a vacancy, turn in annual evaluation forms or submit documentation of underperformance. The average HR employee working in a school district in the United States is not a trained educator or leader and does not have a deep understanding of the skills, knowledge and behaviors needed to effectively facilitate the work of teaching and learning. Far too often, the work of human resources personnel is not connected to student performance outcomes or school improvement plans. If we as educators are going to meet the needs of our students, HR professionals and education leaders must begin working in partnership to provide strategic talent leadership. If we don't, we risk becoming ineffective and ultimately, irrelevant.

In recent years, workforce trends across the nation and within the field of education have experienced seismic shifts, forcing HR departments to rethink their role and their relationship with principals. Nationally, our field has experienced a 35 percent decline in the number of candidates enrolling in teacher education programs between the years 2009 and 2014 (Sutcher, Darling-Hammond, & Carver-Thomas, 2016). Our first challenge is keeping the pipeline from preparation to certification robust. An added challenge is that students entering the teaching profession have lower average SAT scores than their nonteaching counterparts (Goldhaber, 2013), an indication that education is no longer attracting the brightest candidates to prepare our next generation of learners. Goldhaber's findings may explain why teacher salaries have remained about 20 percent lower than their college educated peers working in other fields (Allegretto, 2018). These reports indicate that principals have a smaller candidate pool from which to choose and that the candidates in that pool may not possess the cognitive horsepower they once did. Unfortunately, the challenges do not end there.

The U.S. Department of Labor estimates that by the age of 38, today's learners will have between eight and ten jobs (U.S. Department of Labor, 2018). Over the course of their early career, they will change jobs every two years! Annually, 33 percent of workers in the United States change jobs each year and at any given time, 50 percent are seeking out new employment opportunities (Gallup, 2018). Millenials and Gen Z'ers are not entering the workforce with plans to affiliate with and retire from the same company. These challenges are forcing HR departments in school districts across the county to problem solve these and other barriers to acquiring, accelerating and advancing a quality educator workforce capable of improving academic and nonacademic outcomes for students. In today's uncertain and changing environment, human resource departments can no longer ignore that they must partner with school leaders, and districts can no long ignore that they need to support their principals in becoming strategic talent leaders.

Strategic talent leadership can be developed through the adoption of a comprehensive and aligned talent development strategy. It is no longer sufficient to rely upon recruiting effective educators and hoping that they will remain until retirement. Seventeen percent of teachers leave within their first five years (Gray & Taie, 2015). We must think more strategically about sustaining the educator life cycle if we are going to cultivate the talents of prospective and current educators. That is the purpose of this book. Whereas many books address individual components of talent leadership (e.g., recruiting, onboarding, coaching, retaining), this text describes a comprehensive system of strategic talent leadership practices and tools designed to work in alignment to achieve exponential results. Research suggests that 'strategic alignment' or coordination of various human capital functions is a strong predictor of an organization's performance (Becker, Ulrich, & Huselid et al., 2001). It is with student outcomes and performance in mind that the primary purpose of this book is to provide education leaders with a framework for aligning educator talent practices, tools and assessments with the end goal of becoming strategic talent leaders.

The Strategic Talent Leadership Framework

This introductory chapter provides a brief overview of the domains and functions that makeup the Strategic Talent Leadership Framework (STLF, Figure 1). The four talent domains correspond to the life cycle of any educator role (not career) whether a beginning teacher, first-year principal or promotion into a new position of greater scope and influence. Within each of the four domains are three strategic functions. Each function is linked to research-based best practices, progress-monitored talent analytics and tools to maximize outcomes. While individual functions can operate

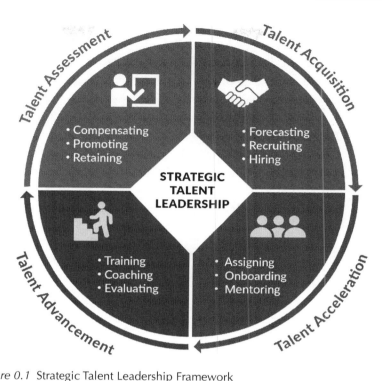

Figure 0.1 Strategic Talent Leadership Framework

and be measured in isolation, the STLF is meant to be used as a system. When all domains and functions are used in alignment, organizations can transform their talent landscape and improve student outcomes.

Talent Acquisition is the first domain in the STLF. This domain encompasses the work of forecasting future vacancies, recruiting to fill those vacancies and the processes that lead to selecting and hiring the best candidates. Success in this domain drives all other domains. As the old adage says, 'Garbage in, garbage out.' Poor choices made at the acquisition stage limit the potential of all other domains to achieve desired outcomes. Well-made decisions in this first stage, however, can fast-track all other efforts to foster educator talent.

The functions of the second domain, Talent Acceleration, shorten the learning curve that occurs after initial hire or promotion into a new role. The strategic placement or assignment of an educator into the right role can greatly increase the chances for success. Paired with a strong onboarding program and ongoing mentoring, these three functions lead to increased retention, job satisfaction and engagement. When talent is accelerated, employees are quickly acculturated and have great clarity about their role within the organization and what is expected of them in that role. Sadly, this is often an overlooked talent domain, especially for educators who are promoted into a role of greater scope and influence. Embarking upon a new journey without a road map leads to frustration, inefficiency, and in many cases, unnecessary attrition. Strategic acceleration efforts can mitigate these undesirable outcomes.

Domain three, Talent Advancement, is a critical driver of overall organizational development. There are only two ways to increase the talent resources of an organization. You can add educators with a proven track record onto an existing team, or you can develop the talents of existing employees. In both cases, the continuous advancement of educator skills and knowledge is necessary. Training, coaching and evaluative feedback are key strategies for advancing individual educator talents. As Baby Boomers and Gen X'ers are replaced with Millenials and Gen Z'ers, workforce engagement and opportunities to develop professionally are more in demand. In 2018, 63 percent of organizations reported having 'future of work' program that prepared employees for future roles, some of which were not yet defined (Leddy, 2018). When executed in alignment with future staffing needs, training, coaching and evaluation activities prepare educators for promotion opportunities. More importantly, advancement activities strengthen the overall talent pool of the organization, creating a reserve pool of skills and knowledge that enable an organization to quickly respond to unforeseen future needs.

Talent Assessment, although the final domain in the framework, is actually the ongoing process of monitoring the bench strength of your organization. Assessment is placed as the fourth domain in the framework because gaps identified in this domain serve to drive talent acquisition efforts in the first phase of the talent cycle. The process of assessing talent includes aligning monetary and non-monetary compensation to roles based upon scope of influence and impact within the organization. Further, it requires succession planning to identify talent for promotion opportunities while simultaneously leveraging smart retention strategies to ensure talent availability to achieve organizational priorities. Active retention practices can prevent the destabilization of teams and faculty as well as preserving the total body of an organization's talent. When an organization retains talent, it is easier to gain momentum in achieving organizational and academic goals. As the organization continues to develop and grow, the talent cycle begins again as educators are acquired for new roles, accelerated in those new roles, advanced and continuously assessed for future roles. In total, the 4 domains and 12 functions are a comprehensive framework for thinking about and making actionable strategic talent leadership for school improvement.

How to Use This Book

This book is designed to support the transformation of educators into strategic talent leaders. Superintendents will discover both policy recommendations and strategic plan initiatives that, if put into action, can support organizational development. For human resource departments, this book is a step-by-step guide to assessing current practice and supporting the transition from a transactional to a transformational service provider. Principal supervisors and principals will find this book to be a toolkit for becoming strategic talent leaders. Colleges and universities seeking a practical guide for teaching strategic talent leadership can use this text to develop principal and superintendent licensure candidates into strategic talent leaders. Accessible to a wide audience, this book is designed to be not only a guide, but a toolkit for putting research into practice. As such, it is organized with the practicing educator in mind.

The STLF is the overall structure for this text. Each book section focuses upon one talent domain and includes three chapters, each of which highlights one talent function. Within each chapter, readers will find the below features:

- Case Scenarios that illustrate the importance of the talent function

- Research from education and corporate fields that supports specific and impactful practices in strategic talent leadership

- Strategic Talent Leadership Insight survey questions that will help to determine current areas of talent leadership strength and possible next steps

- Best Practices and policies that will strengthen leadership within that talent function

- Strategic Talent Leadership Tools for applying one of the best practices

- Action Steps Planner for reflecting upon what enhancements, abandonments or changes to be made to strengthen talent leadership
- Talent Analytics that identify the metrics that will aid in collecting, interpreting and monitoring progress and performance
- Case Study Reflections to help you, as the reader, consider how you would respond to the real-life scenario presented at the start of the chapter

In addition to these chapter features, the Appendix is filled with additional resources to help put all recommended practices into action. Using the Strategic Talent Leadership Site-Based Assessment, principals can assess their current talent strategy against research-based best practices. Once this baseline data is collected, the Strategic Talent Leadership Action Plan can aid in prioritizing next steps, mapping out a change timeline and even help to think through the allocation of resources necessary to achieve improved outcomes. The Strategic Talent Leadership Scorecard includes all "Talent Analytics" from the book chapters that should be used to measure continuous progress and impact to inform future strategy. In support of progress, the Strategic Talent Leadership Toolkit is provided as blank masters that can be duplicated, modified and used in your organization to enact best practices. The use of these tools, in alignment with the STLF, will support educators in becoming strategic talent leaders and ultimately improve outcomes for all students. Finally, the Strategic Talent Leadership Calendar will help practitioners to know what to focus on and when as they progress through the academic year.

The recommended approach to putting the STLF and all of its resources into action is to identify a Strategic Talent Leadership Team to read this book in its entirety. After an initial read, it is recommended that teams administer the Strategic Talent Leadership Site-Based Assessment to establish a baseline of their current practices. Once this data is collected, the Strategic Talent Leadership Team should prioritize next steps in one or more of the talent functions. For teams that are particularly weak in current practices, it is strongly recommended that they begin with Domain I-Talent Acquisition, as this will yield higher-caliber educators who will serve to strengthen practice in other areas. As new practices are implemented, teams should continue the use of the Strategic Talent Leadership Scorecard to track progress. The scorecard should be revisited on a quarterly basis, always informing practice and next steps until all 4 domains and all 12 talent functions are fully aligned.

As with any change effort, the initial work is the hardest. But, once momentum builds and results start rolling in, the talent landscape of your organization will forever be changed!

References

Allegretto, S. (2018). *The teacher pay penalty has hit a new high*. Retrieved from Economic Policy Institute: https://www.epi.org/publication/teacher-pay-gap-2018/

Becker, B., Ulrich, D., & Huselid, M. A. (2001). *The HR scorecard: Linking people, strategy, and performance*. Cambridge, MA: Harvard Business School Press Books.

Gallup. (2018). *The State of the American Workforce 2018*. Gallup.

Goldhaber, D. (2013). Rhetoric versus reality: Is the academic caliber of the teacher workforce changing? *CEDR Working Paper*. Seattle, WA.

Gray, L., & Taie, S. (2015). *Public school teacher attrition and mobility in the first five years: Results from the first through fifth waves of the 2007–08 beginning teacher longitudinal study (NCES 2015-337)*. U.S. Department of Education. Washington, DC: National Center for Education Statistics. Retrieved from http://nces.ed.gov/pubsearch.

Hattie, J. (2011). *Visible learning for teachers*. New York: Routledge.

Konoske-Graf, A., Partelow, L., & Benner, M. (2016). *To attract great teachers, school districts must improve their human capital systems*. Washington, DC: Center for American Progress. Retrieved from https://www.americanprogress.org/issues/education-k-12/reports/2016/12/22/295574/to-attract-great-teachers-school-districts-must-improve-their-human-capital-systems/

Leddy, C. (2018). *Reimagining Work 20/20*. Catalent Technologies.

National Center for Education Statistics. (2018). *Digest of education statistics*. Retrieved from: https://nces.ed.gov/programs/digest/d18/tables/dt18_236.20.asp?current=yes

RAND Education. (2012). *Teachers matter: Understanding teachers' impact on student achievement*. Santa Monica: RAND Corporation.

Sutcher, L., Darling-Hammond, L., & Carver-Thomas, D. (2016). *A coming crisis in teaching? Teacher supply, demand, and shortages in the U.S.* Washington, DC: Learning Policy Institute.

U.S. Department of Labor. (2018). *Futurework Report*. U.S. Department of Labor.

Talent Acquisition

Talent Acquisition

- Forecasting
- Recruiting
- Hiring

Forecasting

With another school year successfully wrapped up, Principal Hopkins was looking forward to a relaxing tour of three national parks with her family. It was a bucket list trip that she was finally checking off! Refreshed and full of energy, she returned to find three retirement letters on her desk, each from one of her star teachers. She knew that each had many years of experience but did not realize they were all eligible for retirement. The last district job fair of the season was the previous week. She left for her trip fully staffed, but came back needing to fill three critical positions. Principal Hopkins was now facing the last weeks of the summer with all of the best candidates already taken.

Forecasting Talent

Forecasting is the practice of using historical data to predict future vacancies. When principals have knowledge of future vacancies, they can proactively seek out the very best candidates, spend appropriate time screening them and make hiring offers early in the recruiting season. There is a direct correlation between a teacher's hire date and level of effectiveness (Levin & Quinn, 2003; Papay & Kraft, 2016). The earlier a teacher is hired, the more effective she/he is once in the classroom. When principals can leverage accurate vacancy forecasts, they can hire early, taking advantage of the strongest candidate pool. It is for that reason that forecasting future staffing needs is an essential function of strategic talent leadership.

In order to accurately forecast needs, principals need access to two sets of historical information—teacher supply data and teacher demand data.

Teacher hiring patterns are driven by the availability of candidates, otherwise known as the 'supply.' Supply data begins with career interest levels among high schoolers and ends with educator preparation program completers at the university level. Aragon (2016) summarized survey data from high school students who took the ACT and the Department of Education to identify interest in pursuing teacher education majors. She identified that from 2010 to 2014, high school student interest in becoming a teacher dropped from 15,595 to 10,678, a 32 percent decrease. This decline in interest directly impacted findings in other studies which described waning enrollment in schools of education.

In parallel, Sutcher, Darling-Hammond, and Carver-Thomas (2016) calculated that between 2009 and 2014, enrollment in educator preparation programs fell 35 percent nationally. The resulting impact was 240,000 fewer teachers available on an annual basis for hiring. This same study estimated a current annual national need of 260,000 newly hired teachers and an annual supply of 196,000. But, this shortage of 64,000 teachers does not impact schools equally. STEM subjects and special education remain hard to staff. Schools in the Southeast, rural areas and high-poverty urban areas continue to have difficulty finding and retaining quality candidates. And, the overall pool of candidates is shrinking, making forecasting even more critical to the effort of securing the best teachers for our students. "However, the problem with staffing may not only be an issue of supply," according to Levin and Quinn (2003), "a district must know in advance that the position will be vacant." Identifying these vacancies early provides districts and principals with projected future needs for teachers by grade level and licensure area.

The second set of information needed to properly forecast is the future need for teachers. Teacher demand patterns are driven by multiple factors—birth rates, the local economy, workforce trends and attrition. As birth rates shift up and down, so does the demand for teachers. Using a staffing ratio of 1:25, an increase in live births by 5,000 in a single district would create a future demand of 200 kindergarten teachers within five years. To know this in advance would be greatly advantageous to a district's recruiting efforts. Likewise, shifts in the local economy and workforce impact teacher demand. A large employer moving their headquarters out of a community could draw hundreds of students away from a school district, whereas a new affordable living community could draw an influx of students. Maintaining close relationships with county commissioners, city councils, the chamber of commerce and local business and industry boards can aid in acquiring early access to information that can influence forecasting decisions. The final data source for teacher demand is held by the district and schools themselves. Teacher attrition is inclusive of migration to other organizations, resignations, retirements and leaves of absence. These data points should be regularly tracked and used to inform forecasting decisions. Ultimately, forecasting should not only include estimates of overall teacher needs, but reporting should break down those needs by school, grade level, licensure area and even identify special knowledge areas or skill sets necessary to improve student outcomes.

Strategic Talent Leadership Insights for Forecasting

With your Strategic Talent Leadership Team, review the strategic talent leadership practices for forecasting (see Table 1.1). If you are currently engaging in a practice, check 'yes.' If not, check 'not yet' and consider how

Table 1.1 Strategic Talent Leadership Insights for Forecasting

Strategic Practice	Yes	Not Yet
Our organization requires educators to submit nonbinding Declarations of Intent in December of each school year which allows hiring managers the greatest amount of time to plan for new hires.		
Our organization opens up an inter-school transfer window in January for transfers that will go into effect the following school year.		
Our organization requires educators to initiate the retirement process at least 6 months in advance of the retirement date.		
Our organization tracks annual birth rate data to inform future kindergarten cohort enrollment which drives fluctuations in the number of teacher positions needed.		
Our organization tracks historical attrition data to forecast future hiring needs.		

this practice could be adopted by your organization as you read through the best practices described in this chapter.

Best Practices for Forecasting Talent

Lengthen the Runway

Most school districts struggle to navigate the multiple deadlines that impact their ability to accurately forecast staffing needs and provide principals enough 'runway' to recruit and hire top candidates. These include but are not limited to (a) local and state budget deadlines which most often operate with a fiscal year start date of July 1 and federal budget deadlines which operate with a fiscal year start date of October 1; (b) district interschool transfer policies and deadlines; (c) district and state resignation policies and deadlines; (d) district and state retirement policies and deadlines; (e) district Individualized Education Plan (IEP) completion deadlines that allow for special education services to be translated into full-time equivalent positions for the upcoming school year; (f) the provision of staffing allocations to principals. Ideally, all decisions and deadlines that impact forecasting would be made by December of each school year, allowing districts to provide principals with the next school year's staffing allocations in January. But, that is not a realistic expectation, as many deadlines reside outside the control of local school boards. Best practice for aligning deadlines is to advance all locally controlled decisions to occur as early in the school year as is possible, creating the longest possible runway for forecasting, recruiting and hiring while adjusting numbers as additional information becomes available. As Voltaire warned, 'the best is the enemy of the good.'

Strategic Transfer Policies

District transfer policies vary widely and may be dependent upon union negotiations. To the extent that transfer policies are within local control and/or negotiation, principals should advocate for transfers to be limited to between-school-year time periods. 'Always open' transfer policies should be discouraged as during the school year attrition can be disruptive to student learning. Strategic transfer policies will open a window for transfers to be secured early in the school year, for example, in January, with movement to occur after the school year ends. This timeline allows for principals to leverage strong candidate pools throughout the spring to fill transfer-out positions. Transfer polices that allow movement into the late spring, or even into summer, only serve to further disadvantage students in hard-to-staff schools. Considerations should include limiting the number or percentage of teachers transferring out of a single school. This cap may be set lower for hard-to-staff schools in order to protect the stability of the faculty and momentum of school improvement efforts. Additionally, equitable distribution of teacher quality should be considered when approving transfers. Protecting our most fragile students from the negative impacts of teacher migration will, in the long run, support improved student outcomes.

Retirement Notification Incentives

Annually, retirements account for 31 percent of teacher attrition (Sutcher et al., 2016). As an example, in a large district with 5,000 teachers and an annual attrition rate of 12 percent, approximately 186 of those teachers are potential retirements. Recruiting and hiring 186 teachers is extremely time intensive and early knowledge of these retirements, the grade level and licensure areas would be extremely valuable to any district and principal. Putting into place a policy requiring a six-month advance retirement notification would allow principals a time advantage for securing candidates to fill these future vacancies. If instituting such a policy is not allowable in your organization, consider offering a monetary incentive, such as a $500 spot bonus, to employees who voluntarily submit their notification six months in advance of their retirement. This small, per retiree, investment will allow you to recruit and hire from a much higher-quality candidate pool than if you were seeking to fill 186 positions in July.

Student Birth and Enrollment Trends

One of the most stable data sources for forecasting future staffing needs is your region's live birth rates. Annually, the Center for Disease Control

(CDC) publishes a live birth rate report that can be used to project out the number of kindergarteners that will enroll in five years. Local municipalities will also have this data and can likely break this data down even further by zip code, gender, ethnicity, socio-economic status (SES), etc. Using historical birth and enrollment rates, superintendents and principals can project out the percentage of births that translate into enrolled students. For example, one principal I worked with explained to me that he could look at the number of births for any given year and know that 25 percent of that number would equal his kindergarten class five years forward. Tracking historical cohort enrollment in kindergarten can then be used to project grade-level enrollment through high school on an annual basis. While other factors such as the job market, housing market and local economics need to be taken into account, watching birth rate data certainly provides principals with a very strong indicator for forecasting staffing needs.

Track Historical Supply and Demand Data

Knowledge of who is coming into your organization, using hiring patterns, and who is leaving it, using attrition patterns, is a strong data source for forecasting future staffing needs. By examining the sources of your hires over time, you can not only strengthen your forecasting but can better align recruiting efforts to your sources of candidates. Table 1.2 shows historical hiring trends by supply source. Other considerations to take into account are changing state testing requirements which could limit the production of new, in-state candidates, changes in teacher-to-student ratios which could increase your need for teachers and any licensure requirement changes that could tighten or open your pipeline of candidates. With multiple years of hiring data, districts and principals can use a combination of trend data and contextual data to predict staffing needs for future school years.

Similarly, attrition data can reveal the patterns that create annual hiring needs (Table 1.3). Principals who track the reasons for attrition can more accurately predict future staffing needs by grade level and subject area. Knowledge of why teachers are leaving can also arm principals with the knowledge of how to mitigate unnecessary attrition. Chapter 12, Retention, will go into great depth on this topic.

Table 1.2 Sample Historical Hiring Trends by Supply Source

Source	2018–2019	2019–2020	2020–2021	2021–2022 Projections
State college X	7	9	10	11
State university X	13	12	14	12
Out-of-state college X	2	4	4	4
Out-of-state university X	1	0	2	2
In-state experienced from other districts	34	48	39	40
Out-of-State experienced from other districts	9	11	10	10
Alternative certification	45	47	33	42
Total historical hires	111	131	112	121

Whether hiring and attrition data is tracked at the district and/or school level, it is an invaluable source of information for creating accurate forecasting reports that can be used to recruit and hire the very best candidates. With this data, HR departments can create a comprehensive forecast of hiring needs each January for the following school year. Early

Table 1.3 Sample Historical Attrition Trends by Reason

Source	2018–2019	2019–2020	2020–2021	2021–2022 Projections
Retirement	27	24	30	32
Leave of absence	3	5	0	3
Migration to another school or district	20	17	23	20
Resignation from the profession	8	5	8	7
Total historical attrition	58	51	61	62

access to this information provides principals and hiring managers with the information they need to begin recruiting, considering requests for transfers in/out of their school and the impacts of enrollment changes on their staffing needs.

 ## Strategic Talent Leadership Tool 1— The Declaration of Intent

You may have found yourself in a similar position to Principal Hopkins, thinking that you were fully staffed only to discover that you are unexpectedly in need of a teacher. While you can never guarantee that you will be 100 percent staffed on the first day of school despite all of your best efforts, there are strategies you can employ to increase your chances of being so. One of those is to employ the use of Strategic Leadership Tool 1—The Declaration of Intent.

The tool is a very straightforward strategy that can provide rich information about your faculty members' career intentions. Before using the tool, there are some considerations to think through:

- When should you distribute the Declaration of Intent letters?
- How should you distribute the Declaration of Intent letters?
- How will you follow up on the information gathered from the distribution of the Declaration of Intent letters?

Most principals who have used this tool have elected to distribute the Declaration of Intent in January as a part of a faculty meeting during which they explain the purpose of the letter. Prior to distribution, it is important to stress that the letter is not binding; it is merely an expression of a faculty member's intention for the upcoming school year. As the building leader, it is important to be clear about who will have access to the information, once collected, and how it will be used. While up to the individual principal, best practice would be to explain that all intentions will be held confidential by the principal and any assistant/vice-principals for use in creating a staffing forecast for the following school year. Should a completed letter express a desire to move within the school, the principal should commit to having a follow-up conversation with the team member. As the building leader, the most important message you can share is that you appreciate your faculty sharing information with you and that you will honor it by treating it with a level of importance equal to the intent with which it was shared. Figure 1.1 provides a sample Declaration of Intent.

Declaration of Intent

Thank you for considering your career opportunities for the upcoming school year. While it is our goal to retain 100% of our team, we understand that, at times, faculty may leave a school for a promotion, family transfer, leave of absence or other reason. By sharing your nonbinding declaration of intent, you are supporting us in forecasting our future staffing needs and recruiting top educators to join our team. Your response will be held in confidence by the administrative team and will be used only for planning purposes. Should you request a follow-up meeting, please indicate so by checking the box at the bottom of this letter. Thank you for your commitment to our students!

Name: _____

Next school year, I intend to:

☐   Remain at School X in my current position

☐   Remain at School X, but would like to be considered for another position within the school

☐   Transfer to another school or department within the district

☐   Take a leave of absence (FMLA, maternity, disability, etc.)

☐   Retire

☐   Resign to work in another school district

☐   Resign and leave the field of education

Would you like to schedule a follow-up meeting to discuss your future plans with a member of our administrative team?

☐   Yes   ☐   No

Thank you for your response!

Figure 1.1 Declaration of Intent

Table 1.4 Action Steps for Forecasting

Best Practice	Required Resources	Lead	Timeline

Action Steps for Forecasting

With your Talent Development Team, identify next steps in becoming more strategic in your forecasting practices.

- Which best practices are you already using to successfully forecast vacancies?
- Which new practices would you like to begin implementing?
- In Table 1.4, list new practices for implementation, data/resources needed, a lead team member and the timeline for putting your next steps into action.

Talent Analytics for Forecasting

You have now assessed your current practices and identified some action steps. Below are the talent analytics, found in the Strategic Talent Leadership Scorecard (Appendix C), that you can use to measure and track your progress towards being a strategic talent leader.

1. Educator intentions as reported on the Declarations of Intent
2. Educator transfers secured through the interschool transfer process as reported by school
3. Educators eligible for retirement by position and/or school
4. Positions to be added or subtracted based upon changes in student enrollment
5. Positions to be added or subtracted based upon historical attrition patterns

Case Study Response

Now that you have learned more about best practices for forecasting the hiring of educators, what advice would you give to Principal Hopkins? Write your response in the space below:

_____

_____

_____

_____

_____

References

Aragon, S. (2016). *Teacher shortages: What we know*. Denver, CO: The Education Commission of the States.

Levin, J., & Quinn, M. (2003). *Missed opportunities: How we keep high quality teachers out of urban classrooms*. New York, NY: The New Teacher Project. Retrieved from: https://tntp.org/assets/documents/MissedOpportunities.pdf

Papay, J., & Kraft, M. (2016). The productivity costs of inefficient hiring practices: Evidence from late teacher hiring. *Journal of Public Policy and Management, 35*(4), pp. 791–817.

Sutcher, L., Darling-Hammond, L., & Carver-Thomas, D. (2016). *A coming crisis in teaching? Teacher supply, demand, and shortages in the U.S.* Washington, DC: Learning Policy Institute.

Recruiting

It was June 1st and the recruiting team from Mt. Pleasant Independent School District had 167 vacancies to fill before August 15th, the first teacher workday of the next school year. The applicant pool was robust at 400 applications. The team felt good about their ability to fill all of the vacancies with top talent and opening the school year fully staffed! The next week, students let out and principals began pouring into the HR office, reviewing applications so that they could begin scheduling interviews. Then it started ... principal after principal began calling Dr. Peeples, the HR Director, complaining that the applicants they called were reporting that their applications were a year old, that they had already accepted other offers or that they had moved out of state. Other principals were frustrated that out of the 400 applications, only two were for secondary math and only six for high school science. The applicant pool was deceiving. While large in numbers, it was not populated with the right candidates or viable candidates. The principals of Mt. Pleasant ISD were looking at an eight-week summertime window to recruit, screen, hire and onboard 167 candidates.

Recruiting Talent

Strategic forecasting practices will provide principals and hiring managers with the student enrollment and staffing allocation data needed in order to begin recruiting the right candidates from the best sources. Well-prepared with this information, recruiting efforts can be targeted and highly productive, yielding top talent. Ideally, all forecasting should be completed by January prior to the following school year and used to drive strategic recruiting efforts.

Recruiting is the practice of marketing your organization to targeted audiences. Done well, recruiting helps to build your organization's image and reputation as being a preferred place to work. A strong recruiting plan includes varied efforts such as building relationships with traditional educator preparation programs, partnerships with alterative certification programs, leveraging teacher exchange organizations, social media campaigns, strong marketing strategies, internal ambassadors and teacher production aligned recruiting budgets. A multipronged strategy offers protection against the loss of a single source of candidates should it cease to be productive. When districts embrace robust recruiting techniques, they ensure principals' access to the top echelon of candidates. Educator quality is crucial to improved student outcomes, which is why recruiting is a practice of all strategic talent leaders.

Strategic talent leaders see themselves as talent scouts for their schools. Sadly, I've recruited far too many teachers in restaurants by engaging my server in conversation only to find out that they were full-time teachers who were waiting tables at night. As many as one-third of teachers work a second job in order to meet budget (Walker, 2019; Will, 2019) and can be found working in restaurants, tutoring centers, hotels, retail and other places that employ shift workers that allow teachers to work after the school day and on weekends. Strategic principals, whether they are attending regional trainings, community events (I once recruited a teacher at a 4th of July celebration), fundraisers, conferences or are out to dinner with friends, are always on the lookout for great people to join their team. They collect resumes and references year-round. When a vacancy arises, strategic principals email these contacts, informing them of upcoming opportunities and ask if they know of anyone who might be a good match.

A fierce commitment to continuous recruiting is a necessary part of building the most effective team of educators for your students. Higher-achieving schools tend to attract more effective teachers, whereas lower-performing schools experience great difficulty (Loeb, Beteille, & Kalogrides, 2012). Principals of schools that are not yet high achieving need, therefore, to be even more aggressive about selling their schools and securing top candidates early in the hiring season. The biggest challenge in doing this is allocating the effort and attention at the right time of the year that it takes to secure talent for your school.

Not investing in recruiting at the right time of the school year can further complicate efforts to improve student outcomes. Levin and Quinn (2003) documented the behaviors of teacher candidates who withdrew from the hiring process. In the organizations they studied, between 31 and 60 percent of applicants self-selected out because they were never contacted with a job offer from their preferred employer. Instead, these candidates who had "significantly higher GPAs and were 40 percent more likely to have a degree in their teaching field" (Levin & Quinn, 2003) accepted teaching jobs with other districts. A lack of time invested in these candidates resulted in the hire of lower-quality candidates, making it even more difficult to reach school improvement goals. There are, however, several strategies districts and principals can leverage year-round to ensure the acquisition of the best talent for students.

Strategic Talent Leadership Insights for Recruiting

With your Strategic Talent Leadership Team, review the strategic talent leadership practices for recruiting (see Table 2.1). If you are currently engaging in a practice, check 'yes.' If not, check 'not yet' and consider how this

Table 2.1 Strategic Talent Leadership Insights for Recruiting

Strategic Practice	Yes	Not Yet
Our organization currently recruits from multiple candidate sources to ensure a strong pipeline of candidates. (Examples: Universities, Grow Your Own Programs, Teach for America, Alternative Certification, Troops to Teachers, Teacher Cadets)		
Our organization uses a pipeline tracker so that principals and hiring managers always have access to current recruiting information.		
Our organization uses an employee ambassador program to reward referrals that lead to the hire of a new employee.		
Our organization maintains a list of highly effective employees eligible for a returnship (retirees or employees who left the district in good standing who are eligible for re-employment).		
Our organization offers incentives such as early contracts and/or signing bonuses to candidates in hard-to-staff positions.		

practice could be adopted by your organization as you read through the best practices described in this chapter.

Best Practices for Recruiting Talent

Diversify Your Sources

Just as with monetary investments, principals and districts should maintain a diverse portfolio of sources from which to recruit. If one industry (or educator preparation source) dries up, the remaining sources can continue to fill the talent pipeline needed to staff all vacancies. A recent example of this is a university whose enrollment in special education was so low that the school had to cut the program, eliminating the only source of special education teachers for a local school district. Recruiting from multiple pathways—traditional, alternative certification, teacher exchange organizations, Teach for America, TNTP, residency programs, in and out-of-state transfers and boomerang teachers (those that resign or retire and come back)—will ensure a stable pipeline. Other sources include:

Student Teachers: One of the best sources of candidates is the student teacher currently in residence in your own schools. They are unique candidates in that, depending upon the educator preparation program, principals and hiring managers have the ability to observe their practice within their own schools and organizational context, working with their own students and using district approved curricula. Additionally, student teachers have already begun to form relationships with peer teachers, supervising teachers, administrations, parents and students, making them more likely to want to continue the existing momentum of teaching in-district. Do not hesitate to aggressively recruit the student teachers in your schools as they are likely the lowest cost-per-recruit option for your organization.

Teacher Cadets: Establish a Teacher Cadets Program or Future Educators of America club in your high schools. Working with local foundations and business partners, arrange to pay for the college expenses of candidates who agree to return to your school system and teach under a memorandum of understanding for an agreed-upon number of years.

Grow Your Own: Within your state licensure guidelines, establish your own teacher residency program. Candidates for this program can be existing teacher assistants, classified personnel or local professionals interested in a career change. Many states allow in-district licensure programs to provide candidates with existing bachelor's degrees the opportunity to obtain licensure through significant locally provided training and supervised teaching experiences. One such program is Guilford County Schools' (Greensboro, NC) GCS-Alternative Certification Track which has prepared almost 500 teachers for licensure. Their graduates, many of whom held masters and doctoral degrees in STEM fields, are teaching in highly impacted schools with great success. This source of educators has helped to ensure the district 100 percent staffing on the first day of school since its inception.

GIG Economy: Not all teaching jobs have to be full time. Courses can be broken down into individual 'gigs' which can be contracted out to certified teachers who are retired, working remotely with the ability to teach online or who might want to teach one or two classes per day versus working a full-time job. With teacher shortages looming over many schools, leveraging the gig economy model should be a strong consideration—we've been doing it for years in the form of substitute teachers! This model represents a large cost-saving opportunity in that districts would not have to pay for benefits.

Institute of Higher Education (IHE) Partnerships: Not only will strong recruiting strategies include the tracking of future graduates by licensure and graduation year by institute of higher education, the best recruiting strategies will establish partnerships that ensure a robust supply of graduates. Partnerships allow districts to target specific populations of candidates that match their needs (Luczak, Vaishnav, Horwath, & Sanghani, 2016). For example, many schools are seeking to recruit teacher candidates to mirror the diversity of their own student population. Nationally, more than 50 percent of students are non-white, but only 20 percent of teachers in the United States are racially diverse (Meckler & Rabinowitz, 2019). By establishing partnerships with Historically Black Colleges and Universities (HBCUs) and Hispanic Serving Institutions (HSIs), districts can begin to build bridges into their organization for the exact candidates they seek to recruit. Similar partnerships can be designed around specific curriculum programs such as special education, STEM and any other specialized areas sought after by the district. Additionally, districts can work with IHEs to encourage students to double major/double license, increasing their ability to recruit candidates for multiple roles. Ultimately, tracking the return on your program source investment will help you to target the sources that are most productive for your hiring.

Pipeline Tracker

A full recruitment pipeline is the result of a robust marketing and recruiting strategy. Multipronged marketing approaches should leverage social media, the district's website, school tours, job fairs, billboards, radio spots, guest speakers and other opportunities. Ninety-four percent of districts post job openings on their district websites, but only 30 percent of districts post job openings on social media networks" (Konoske-Graf, Partelow, & Benner, 2016), representing a missed opportunity to increase the number of applications per vacancy. Many civic clubs invite experts to attend meetings and talk about the state of their industry. Guest speaking at such an event is an opportunity to not only shape your district's external reputation but to let your community know that you are looking for excellent candidates. Other ways to inform the public about opportunities include taking advantage of free billboard space or radio spots that are donated to the district by local businesses that need to fill air time. Ask your local movie theatre for free ad placement before movies as well. They get a tax write-off and you get free advertising.

All of these activities will help to fill the pipeline, but if applicant engagement is not tracked once candidates apply, it doesn't matter if you have ten applicants or a thousand. Tracking your candidates throughout your recruiting pipeline is crucial. If the recruitment team at Mt. Pleasant ISD had known the number of applicants per vacancy and the qualifications of those applicants, and had tracked how many had been interviewed, they may not be facing 167 vacancies in June. Current and accurate data about your applicants is crucial. Even more important is communicating and engaging with those applicants so that they know where they are in your hiring process. A lack of information can drive a candidate to consider other job offers with other organizations, causing you to lose a potentially high-performing teacher.

Employee Ambassadors

One of the most effective marketing and recruiting strategies available to your organization is internal—your own employees. Within organizations such as schools, up to 80 percent of the perceived value can be attributed to factors driven by the people within the organization itself (Eccles, Newquist, & Schatz, 2007). Therefore, strategic recruiters will identify highly effective and charismatic educators within their organization to serve as brand ambassadors. Once identified and trained to be 'on message' representatives, deploy these ambassadors to job fairs, recruiting events and to host school tours when candidates are exploring their future employment options. Offer employees incentives for referring candidates that become employed. I've often come across human resource leaders that lament their lack of recruiters. And, this is an issue. The Center for American Progress (2016) found that on average, school districts have one recruiter for every 2,000 enrolled students. What they don't realize is that their schools are full of recruiters! Teachers believe, value and listen to other teachers. Let your teachers sell their authentic stories to other teachers. By incenting (through a small monetary reward or just recognition) employees to recruit other great educators into your district, you are strengthening your brand and extending the reach of your recruiting efforts.

Returnships

Boomerang teachers, or those who have returned after being on a leave of absence, working for another organization or who come out of retirement, are an ideal source from which to recruit. By offering Returnships, you are securing experienced educators with track records that can be reviewed to predetermine effectiveness levels. Because they are returning to your school or district, they are already familiar with the organizational history that can represent a learning curve for brand-new teachers. While states have different laws that regulate returning to teacher after a leave of absence or retirement, leveraging this source of educators within these parameters can represent low-hanging fruit in the world of recruiting.

Strategic recruiters will keep a database of potential returnship candidates by licensure area, including those licensed as principals and superintendents. This source of candidates can be activated not only for full-time positions but also to fill long-term leaves of absence, to bridge midyear vacancies into the next school year or to substitute in critical need areas. Depending upon the policies of your district, county or state, returnees may already be receiving health benefits through their retirement plan, making them a less expensive option for filling a vacancy. Many organizations fail to capitalize upon the known entity of these talented educators who may be willing to return and continue serving the students of your district.

Hard-to-Staff Position Incentives

Many factors can impact a principal's ability to recruit top talent to his/her school. Salaries, class size, school demographics, school safety, location and most importantly, working conditions, all play a role in candidates' choices (Aragon, 2016). Even in schools that are not traditionally hard-to-staff, there are positions that remain difficult to fill. Across the nation, STEM and special education remain areas of teacher shortage (Goldhaber & Walch, 2014). In the Southeast, elementary teachers are becoming increasingly difficult to recruit.

In order to mitigate these shortages, districts and schools have developed incentives in alignment to their strategic goals. For some, signing bonuses for accepting early contracts have been sufficient to attract candidates to sign on. In other cases, tiered salary structures that pay STEM and special education teachers at higher rates than their peers have been successful in the recruiting process. More robust models offer both recruitment and performance incentives as well as a range of other tools and supports that create a total compensation package that is highly attractive to educators (Grier & Holcombe, 2008; Holcombe, 2010). A large district in the Southeast, after going an entire year with math vacancies in its most impacted high schools, offered math teachers recruitment bonuses of $10,000, a laptop computer, a smartboard, class sets of graphing calculators, graduate courses in math content and on-site math coaches. When student achievement and growth were achieved at high levels, additional bonuses of $5,000–$12,000 were paid. Over the course of the program, student test scores increased at 100 percent of the high schools and all math vacancies were fully staffed (Holcombe, 2009).

Strategic Talent Leadership Tool 2—Pipeline Tracker

The recruiting team of Mt. Pleasant ISD thought that they had a robust candidate pool with 400 applicants for 167 vacancies. However, they failed to attend to several important factors that lead to quality hires (Table 2.2):

- The number of applications per vacancy
- The number of those applications that were actually eligible to be hired into the role for which they applied (yes, some people apply to every vacancy regardless of their qualifications!)
- Who had and had not been screened or interviewed
- The number of those interviewed that were actually recommended for hire within the district
- The ratio of offers accepted to offers rejected (an indication of your organization's reputation)

If the team had forecasting data available, they could have fed it into a pipeline tracker to match up vacancies with applications, resulting in rich information about progress toward successful hire. There are several software programs that manage forecasting, recruiting and hiring data electronically, making it easy to generate reports that provide quick summaries and snapshots of the HR process. For those teams wishing to adopt the practice of tracking data through a pipeline that do not already use applicant

Table 2.2 Strategic Talent Leadership Tool 2—Pipeline Tracker

Position	School	Applicants	Eligible	Interviewed	Recommended for Hire	Offer Made	Offer Accepted	Offer Rejected
Physics	Washington High School	1	1	1	1	1	0	1
Geometry	Levi High School	0	0	0	0	0	0	0
History	Carver High School	15	10	5	3	1	1	0
Maths	Lincoln Middle School	2	1	1	1	1	1	0
Language Arts	Lincoln Middle School	11	9	5	2	1	1	0
Art	Jackson Middle School	19	15	5	5	1	1	0
Elementary	Sunset Elementary	23	20	5	4	2	1	1
ESL	Green Elementary School	5	3	3	0	0	0	0
Counselor	Northern Elementary School	8	5	5	4	2	1	1

tracking software, a pipeline tracker can easily be developed using a word processing, spreadsheet, database program or even a data wall on a white board. No matter which technology is used, the strategy should:

1. Identify forecasted vacancies by school and list them in the pipeline tracker. Some organizations even assign a hiring manager or recruiter to positions by grade level or licensure area.

2. Match applications to vacancies by tracking the number of applications for each position.

3. Within human resources, have a licensure specialist review the application for eligibility to be hired into the position. At a minimum, this could be licensure and at a maximum, it could include locally imposed qualifications for hire such as grade point average (GPA), recommendations, years of experience and so on. Typically, the number of applicants eligible is smaller than the total number of applicants for the vacancy.

4. Next, eligible candidates should be screened or interviewed for the position. Again, depending upon the size of your organization, this is sometimes done at the district level and other times, by principals at the school level. Regardless, applicants interviewed should be tracked so that principals and hiring managers do not duplicate efforts.

5. The next step in tracking the pipeline is crucial. While five candidates might be interviewed for one position, all might be top applicants who are viable for other vacancies within the district. For that reason, it is important to know which candidates are recommended for hire and employment within the district.

6. Finally, strategic recruiters will track which candidates are made offers, accept offers and reject offers. This will serve as an indicator of your reputation as a district. Ideally, every offer made should be accepted.

Timely communications should parallel the entire pipeline tracking process. If an application is reviewed and found to be eligible, the candidate should receive a communication informing them of such. Likewise, if found ineligible for the position, the candidate should receive a communication letting them know that they are not eligible to be hired for the vacancy.

Table 2.3 Action Steps for Recruiting

Best Practice	Data/Resources	Lead	Timeline

Each step of the recruiting and screening process should include the candidate knowing his/her status. By keeping candidates 'warm' and engaged in the recruiting process, they are more likely to remain interested in and accept a position within your organization. In the next chapter, Hiring, you will learn strategies for screening/interviewing candidates using another tool, the Standards-Based Interview Protocol.

Action Steps for Recruiting

With your Talent Development Team, identify next steps in becoming more strategic in your recruiting practices.

- Which best practices are you already using to successfully recruit talent?
- Which new practices would you like to begin implementing?
- In Table 2.3, list new practices for implementation, data/resources needed, a lead team member and the timeline for putting your next steps into action.

Talent Analytics for Recruiting

You have now assessed your current practices and identified some action steps. Below are the talent analytics, found in the Strategic Talent Leadership Scorecard (Appendix C), that you can use to measure and track your progress toward being a strategic talent leader.

1. The number and licensure area of candidates available from each hiring source

2. Applicant engagement as measured by a pipeline tracker

3. The number of active employee ambassadors and their recruiting results

4. The number and licensure areas of employees eligible for returnships

5. The number and type of incentives offered to candidates in hard-to-staff positions

Case Study Response

Now that you have learned more about best practices for recruiting educators, what advice would you give to the human resources team in Mt. Pleasant? Write your response in the space below:

_____

_____

_____

_____

_____

References

Aragon, S. (2016). *Teacher shortages: What we know*. Education Commission of the States. http://www.ecs.org/teacher-shortages/

Eccles, R. G., Newquist, S. C., & Schatz, R. (2007). Reputation and its risks. *Harvard Business Review,* 2007, 2. Retrieved from: https://hbr.org/2007/02/reputation-and-its-risks

Goldhaber, D., & Walch, J. (2014). Gains in teacher quality: Academic capabilities of the U.S. teaching force are on the rise. *Education Next, 14*(1). Retrieved from: https://www.educationnext.org/gains-in-teacher-quality/

Grier, T., & Holcombe, A. (2008). Mission possible: A North Carolina school district solves the problem of recruiting and retaining teachers in its most challenging schools. *Educational Leadership, 65*(7), pp. 25–30.

Holcombe, A. (2009). More than the sum of its parts. *Principal Leadership, 9*(7), pp. 32–36.

Holcombe, A. (2010). Experiences of an early adopter of incentive pay. *The School Administrator, 3*(67), pp. 16–17.

Konoske-Graf, A., Partelow, L., & Benner, M. (2016). To attract great teachers, school districts must improve their human capital systems. *The Center for American Progress.* Retrieved from: https://www.americanprogress.org/issues/education-k-12/reports/2016/12/22/295574/to-attract-great-teachers-school-districts-must-improve-their-human-capital-systems/

Levin, J., & Quinn, M. (2003). *Missed opportunities: How we keep high quality teachers out of urban classrooms.* New York, NY: The New Teacher Project. Retrieved from: https://tntp.org/assets/documents/MissedOpportunities.pdf

Loeb, S., Beteille, T., & Kalogrides, D. (2012). Effective schools: Teacher hiring, assignment, development, and retention. *Education Finance and Policy, 7*(3), pp. 269–304.

Luczak, J., Vaishnav, A., Horwath, B., & Sanghani, P. (2016). *Education First. Ensuring High Quality Teaching Talent: How Strong, Bold Partnerships between School District and Teacher Preparation Programs are Transforming the Teacher Pipeline.* Retrieved from: http://education-first.com/library/publication/ensuring-high-quality-teacher-talent/

Meckler, L. & Rabinowitz, K. (2019). America's schools are more diverse than ever. But the teachers are still mostly white. *The Washington Post,* December, 2019. Retrieved from: https://www.washingtonpost.com/graphics/2019/local/education/teacher-diversity/?utm_campaign=first_reads&utm_medium=Email&utm_source=Ne%E2%80%A6

Walker, T. (2019). Almost one third of teachers take on second jobs. *NEA Today,* July, 2019. Retrieved from: http://neatoday.org/2019/07/25/teachers-second-jobs/

Will, M. (2019). To make ends meet, 1 in 5 teachers have second jobs. *Education Week,* June, 2019. Retrieved from: https://www.edweek.org/ew/articles/2018/06/19/to-make-ends-meet-1-in-5.html

3 | Hiring

Principal Lloyd was proud of her interviewing technique. Instead of using the recommended district hiring protocol which was aligned to the teacher performance standards, she relied upon her 'secret' set of questions that she believed elicited the very core values and beliefs from candidates. Her favorite question … "If you were a color, what color would you be?" She always saved it for last and believed it cinched the interview. Principal Lloyd was pleased that she was able to conduct all of her own hiring without the need for an interview team. She believed that this efficiency enabled her faculty to focus their time in the classroom instead of wasting time sitting in interviews. In her most recent evaluation conference, she expressed frustration with the school's lackluster achievement results. So much of her time was being spent on documenting poor teacher performance. She didn't understand why her teachers were not achieving expected student growth results.

Hiring Talent

Although forecasting and recruiting are essential for attracting the right talent to your organization, hiring is the most crucial function of talent acquisition. Hiring is the practice of using purposeful selection criterion to strategically acquire the best talent possible. How employees are hired sets the precedent for their future relationship with your organization. High standards used during the hiring process sends the message that your school and district has high expectations. Therefore, how a new employee is screened and hired should be in tight alignment with how their future performance will be evaluated. When principals hire based upon the congruence between candidate qualifications and the professional standards by which they will be evaluated once on the job, the employee will experience greater success and job satisfaction. A thoughtful, well-designed hiring strategy yields a high-performing employee and stronger retention rates. It is for these reasons that hiring is a key function of strategic talent leadership.

Unfortunately, most educational leaders are not trained to effectively identify, screen and hire talent. At most, one course in Human Resources Leadership was required in graduate school. If you were lucky, a couple hours of that course *may* have been dedicated to the screening and hiring process. More than likely, the course focused on HR policy and law, not on the art of landing the best candidate. Hiring the right team members is one of the most important tasks of an educational leader. Too often, this critical job is completed in isolation, delegated to a human resources hiring manager, an assistant principal, or even fast-tracked so that attention can be paid to what is perceived as being the more important business of instruction. More than one-third of school districts surveyed in a study by the Center for American Progress found that teacher candidates are not required to interview with a school principal as a basic requirement of securing a job (Konoske-Graf, Partelow, & Benner, 2016). On the contrary, hiring the right talent is the lifeblood of any organization. Adding a new educator to your team can change the trajectory of your school—for good or bad. Hiring the best candidate is not quick work, nor is it easy work. But, it is the work that matters most. The quality of the interview drives the quality of the candidate hired.

Let's pretend you are a restaurant owner who has a vacancy for a head chef. How would you hire for that position? Would you screen resumes and then conduct face to face interviews during which you asked a series of 10–20 questions about their philosophy of cooking? No! Of course not. More than likely, you would want to sample dishes they prepared, review menus they crafted and read online reviews of their previous work in other restaurants. Certainly, you would speak to their previous employers to hear feedback about their prior performance. You would watch your candidate in action and even invite him or her to guest chef for an evening at your restaurant to determine their capacity to succeed with your clientele. Much like a chef, a teacher is charged with creating an experience—albeit a learning experience versus a culinary experience. Yet, just over 10 percent of districts require candidates to teach a sample lesson with students as a part of the hiring process (Konoske-Graf et al., 2016). Across the nation, the typical teacher interview still includes a candidate sitting in front of a hiring manager or interview team and answering a series of questions. Like Principal Lloyd, many principals continue to ask questions that do not get to the heart of prior performance and current capacity. This chapter provides several best practices for hiring talent and Strategic Talent Leadership Tool 3— Standards-Based Interview, all of which will significantly improve your chances of securing your top candidate.

Strategic Talent Leadership Insights for Hiring

With your Strategic Talent Leadership Team, review the strategic talent leadership practices for hiring (see Table 3.1). If you are currently engaging in a practice, check 'yes.' If not, check 'not yet' and consider how this practice could be adopted by your organization as you read through the best practices described in this chapter.

Table 3.1 Strategic Talent Leadership Insights for Hiring

Strategic Practice	Yes	Not Yet
Our organization screens and interviews candidates year-round, using standards-based interview (SBI) protocols, ensuring a diverse talent pool at all times.		
Our organization hires 90% of candidates for the upcoming school year by the end of the current school year.		
Our organization over hires for hard-to-staff positions such as STEM, SPED and ESL.		
Our organization interviews underrepresented candidates for each vacancy.		
Our organization leverages reverse interviews to increase candidate satisfaction with job placement.		

Best Practices for Hiring Talent

Cultivate Your Candidate Pool Year-Round

One of the best ways to ensure a robust pool of candidates is to culti-vate it year-round. While many districts focus on a recruiting and hiring 'season,' strategic talent leaders know that securing top talent is a year-round endeavor that entails continuous recruiting from multiple sources and ongoing screening. Just a few under-accessed sources of candidates include December graduates of educator preparation programs; student teachers who, by some local policies, are allowed to be hired as substitute teachers and transitioned into full-time, licensed teachers upon graduation; educators returning from leave and educators who move into the area due to a partner's job change (very common near military bases). By limiting your interviewing and hiring to the spring, you are missing out on a tal-ented pool of educators.

Hire Early

Securing the best candidate is not the work of magic, rather, a series of best practices that are backed up by data. One of the clearest messages that hiring data sends is that there is a direct correlation between the date of hire and the level of teacher effectiveness. Teachers hired late in the summer and after the start of school achieve significantly lower reading and math scores compared to their early-hire peers (Papay & Kraft, 2016). This is not surprising as the top candidates for any position would be selected first, leaving weaker candidates still searching for jobs at the end of the hiring season. Ideal practice would use strong forecasting to gen-erate a list of anticipated vacancies by January, to have a cultivated pool of recruits that have been screened and are ready for hire and to complete all hiring prior to the end of the current school year in preparation for the next. Unexpected resignations will inevitably occur throughout the summer, no matter how proactive you are at forecasting, recruiting and hiring. But with all known vacancies filled early, you can be more selec-tive with summer hiring, still ensuring that you are bringing top talent into your organization.

Over-Hire

Each year, thousands of teachers start the school year excited about welcoming new students, teaching well-planned lessons and the promise of another opportunity to impact the future. For some, however, the start of the school year brings about the realization that teaching is not what they expected. Unfortunately, this means unanticipated resignations which can be devastating and destabilizing for students and schools alike. These impacts can be mitigated with a simple practice—over-hiring for hard-to-staff positions such as math, science, English as a second or other language and special education. At the district level, hiring managers can be proactive about securing 'backup' teachers in hard-to-staff areas. At the start of the school year over-hired faculty can be deployed as substitute teachers or even an extra set of hands for new teachers until a vacancy arises. By over-hiring, the district ensures that they will be 100 percent staffed on the first day of school and will remain so throughout the year.

Leverage Diversity

Not only does using a diverse interview team improve the quality of hire by bringing multiple perspectives and experiences into the decision-making process, but hiring for diversity can positively impact school culture and student achievement. Multiple studies have concluded that when minority students are taught by at least one teacher of the same race, standardized test scores and attendance improve while suspensions decrease (Egalite, 2015; Holt, 2015). Establishing partnerships with Historically Black Colleges and Universities (HBCUs), Hispanic Association of Colleges and Universities (HACUs) and institutions that graduate diverse student bodies can provide your organization with a source of highly qualified educator candidates. Many of these institutions will actually recruit for you and support you in placing candidates in the right positions.

As a strategic talent leader, part of your role is to ensure that your recruiting and hiring processes does not unknowingly screen-out diverse candidates. Several strategies can be employed to counteract this undesirable outcome:

- Redact candidate names before screening applications
- Leverage the expertise of a diverse team (include a diversity officer if you have one) to review your screening process for potential biases
- Ensure diverse representation on interview teams
- Track the ratio of candidates interviewed to candidates hired by demographics to ensure that implicit biases are revealed

Many larger districts go so far as to track the demographics of students and compare them to the demographics of educators to ensure congruence between the two populations. When this is possible, it is certainly a best practice that is linked to improved outcomes for all students and one that should be leveraged.

Reverse Interview

A job offer is like a marriage proposal. Both parties have to agree to it and it should be mutually beneficial. The typical interview process is one-sided with the hiring team asking questions of the job candidate in an attempt to determine fit. Often, the last minutes of the interview are reserved for the wrap-up question, "What questions do you have of us?" Candidates then begin awkwardly asking questions that were prepared in anticipation of this final interview question. On the ride home, candidates inevitably relax and process the interview, generating the 'I should have said this ...' and the 'I should have asked that ....' The reverse interview is designed to capture that 'on the ride home' processing by giving the candidate an opportunity to have a second conversation during which they get to do the interviewing. A reverse interview does not have to be offered to all candidates; however, it is recommended that all finalists be provided this opportunity to have a reverse interview to ensure a mutually beneficial match prior to the offer of a job. As this occurs after the face-to-face interview, a reverse interview can be conducted on the phone. The opportunity for the candidate to ask more probing questions in a lower-stress environment will allow him or her to get a stronger sense of job and organizational culture fit (Lie, 2005). Long-term, this will increase the chance of the candidate accepting your job offer and remaining in the employment of the organization.

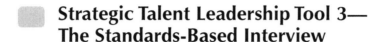

Strategic Talent Leadership Tool 3— The Standards-Based Interview

Principal Lloyd's school district had an interview protocol she could have used. And yet, she continued to lean on her set of questions, refusing to abandon a practice that failed to yield her the top talent she needed to improve outcomes for her students. Like many other hiring managers and principals, she conducted a very typical interview. Principal Lloyd's practice is not very different than that of others. Nationally, the average job interview only lasts 40 minutes (LinkedIn, 2015). If you knew that the teacher candidate you were about to hire would stay in the profession for 30 years, how long would you take to ensure that he or she was the right candidate? I'm guessing more than 40 minutes. You might be thinking that you don't have time to spend three hours interviewing each person who applied for your vacancy and you would be correct. It is for that reason that narrowing down the pool of potential candidates for hire is so important so that you reserve your time to spend with the top two or three candidates using the Standards-Based Interview (SBI). This SBI process consists of three parts: (1) narrowing down the pool, (2) conducting the SBI and (3) making the final job offer.

Step 1 Narrow the Pool

Before you begin using the SBI, you need to narrow down your candidate pool. So, how do you narrow down a candidate pool from the 30 applications you received to the few that you want to interview face to face? The answer is using a screening process (Figure 3.1) that reduces the number of candidates down to those that have a high probability of being the best fit for your school's needs.

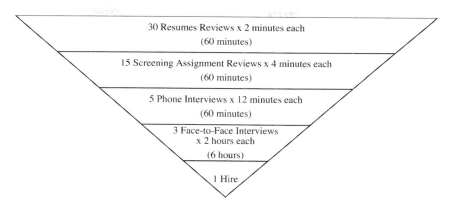

Figure 3.1 Screening Process

Imagine, as in Figure 3.1, that you have a total of 30 candidates that apply for a 4th grade teaching position. You certainly don't have time to spend multiple hours screening each candidate. In fact, you don't even have time to spend 40 minutes with each. By putting into place a screening pipeline process, you can quickly narrow your candidate pool down to a few top candidates, enabling you to use the SBI with just your top candidates. This interview protocol will allow you to spend considerable time with qualified candidates who have already shown a commitment to working in your organization. Following are the phases that will get you from 30 candidates down to your top candidates that will participate in the SBI.

First, briefly review all submitted resumes. At this stage, considered data might include licensure area, grade point average (GPA), criminal history, ability to work legally in the United States, etc. This process will typically reduce your candidate pool by 50 percent which, in this example, would leave you with 15 candidates. Many organizations use an applicant tracking system that uses artificial intelligence (AI), saving the hiring manager a lot of time that would be spent reviewing individual candidate applications. If screening manually, spend no more than two minutes per resume for a total time investment in the first phase is 60 minutes.

Second, now that you have identified the 15 candidates that meet your minimum expectations, send them each a screening assignment via email. This assignment should require enough of a time investment that it will naturally dissuade 'tire kickers' from continuing further in the process while not scaring off your serious contenders. Examples of screening assignments may be to conduct an analysis of a provided set of student data or to develop a lesson plan in response to a provided curriculum standard. Ideally, the screening assignment will take candidates one hour to complete. Those that do not choose to complete the assignment will self-select out of the process, leaving you additional time spend with the serious candidates. Typically, one-third of the candidates will self-select out. If everyone in this example completed the screening assignment (again, highly unlikely), you would yield 15 assignments to review, spending approximately four minutes on each for a total of 60 minutes. From those submitted, select your top third. These are the five candidates that will move on to the next step and receive a phone interview. The total time invested in the second phase is 60 minutes.

Next, the use of a phone interview is a time-saving alternative to a face-to-face interview. A quick, 10-minute personal interaction over the phone can provide significant information about a candidate's professional demeanor, knowledge of the job, willingness to work for your organization and can even be an opportunity for the candidate to determine whether or not she/he remains interested. After conducting your five phone interviews, select your top three candidates to interview face to face. Keep second choice candidates warm in case your top choices do not meet your criterion or none of them accepts the position offered. The total time invested in this third phase is less than 60 minutes. You still have seven hours left to conduct your SBIs.

Step 2 The Standards-Based Interview

Finally, you have narrowed your candidate pool from 30 down to the three people who you know are qualified *and* interested. This is an ideal scenario for both you and the candidates. This is the stage where you want to really invest your time and energy into gathering as much information about your candidates as possible. And, this is where you will use your SBI tool to conduct multi-hour face-to-face interviews. Of the interview hours you budgeted, you still have seven left. Spending two hours with each of three candidates will use six additional hours, still leaving you one additional hour to call references and conduct a background check on your finalist.

You are now ready to use your SBI to conduct an in-depth interview that relies upon multiple measures to inform candidate-to-job fit. Using multiple measures is the best way to predict future job performance and success (Rockoff, Jacob, Kane, & Staiger, 2008). The SBI triangulates the data you consider by drawing evidence from three different indicators of future success:

- Evidence-Based Indicators: Candidate skills and knowledge are assessed through the provision of existing artifacts such as lesson plans, test scores, letters of reference, publications, awards. All evidence-based artifacts are already in existence before the interview.

- Performance-Based Indicators: Candidate skills and knowledge are assessed in real time through observable actions such as teaching a lesson plan, engaging in a simulation, completing a writing assessment or facilitating an activity during the interview.

- Response-Based Indicators: Candidate skills and knowledge are assessed through a series of behavioral-based questions that require written or verbal responses during the interview.

The differentiator in using a SBI is in aligning your indicators of future success to the standards or competencies your organization uses to measure educator effectiveness. Whether you use a widely available model such as Danielson's Framework for Teaching, the Stronge Teacher and Leader Effectiveness Performance Evaluation System, the Marzano Focused Teacher Evaluation Model or one of your own, the SBI protocol can be used to create the components of your face-to-face interview.

As you can see, in Figure 3.2, the three indicators of future success are listed in column one. The top row of the protocol contains your organization's teacher, principal or other job standards. The ultimate goal is to obtain multiple sources of evidence for all standards so that you ensure your final candidate is able to perform the job for which she/he is hired.

To populate the protocol, put each of your standards at the top of the columns. Next, generate the content of each cell by describing the

	Planning and Preparation	Classroom Environment	Instruction	Professional Responsibilities
Evidence Indicators	A student learning assessment that demonstrates congruence with instructional outcomes	A behavior management plan that clearly explains expectations for learning and achievement	A lesson plan that includes activities, assignments, instructional materials and assessment criteria	A newsletter to families that includes information about the instructional program and how families can be involved
Performance Indicators	Provide the candidate with a student data set and ask him/her to create student groupings for maximum learning and explain their choices.	Provide the candidate with a sample classroom floorplan and furniture. Ask him/her to design the learning environment and explain their choices.	Observe the candidate teaching a mini-lesson of their choosing to a group of students. Have them debrief afterwards on what worked and could be improved.	Ask the candidate to participate in a mock parent conference, during which a parent becomes irate. Debrief afterwards.
Response Indicators	As the candidate questions about their knowledge of special education (SPED) students, SPED law, and planning to meet SPED needs.	Ask the candidate questions about different classroom management scenarios and how they would approach each.	Ask the candidate questions about using questioning and discussion techniques to elicit student learning.	Ask the candidate questions about participating in a school and district projects, trainings, and initiatives.

Figure 3.2 Sample Standards-Based Interview Protocol Based Upon Danielson's Framework for Teaching (2009)

evidences, performances and responses that would be indicators of success for each job standard. By using standards-based selection criterion, race, gender and demographic bias are significantly reduced while employee retention is increased (Spencer & Spencer, 1993). To exemplify how the SBI protocol works, Danielson's Framework for Teaching domains have been used in Figure 3.2 as the job-based competencies. Intersections between the three indicators of future success and four job standards have been populated with one sample in each cell.

Ideally, you would form a team that would spend time building out multiple evidences, performance tasks and questions in each cell so that the protocol can be used with consistency across your district while preserving site-based flexibility in creating role-specific interview experiences.

With your SBI protocol populated, you are ready to create your SBI. It is not necessary, nor would it be worthwhile, to incorporate *all* of the components generated in the SBI protocol (in this case, 12). In creating an interview protocol, the goal is to ensure that each indicator and each standard are addressed at least once. In Figure 3.3, although only 8 of 12 possible SBI protocol components are used, each indicator and each standard are addressed a minimum of one time each. The remaining, unused, components can be incorporated into follow-up questions or used in a second interview if needed.

In total, each of the evidence, performance and response indicators for future success were leveraged twice and each of the domains were addressed twice. While only 8 of the 12 SBI protocol building blocks were used, more could have been added. And, the next time the protocol is used to create a SBI, different combinations of blocks can be used to customize the interview to the position. The SBI protocol can be used again and again to customize interviews for multiple positions. Additional evidences, performance tasks and questions can be added to each cell, providing even more options when designing interview protocols for other teaching vacancies. Once developed, schools and districts can adopt the SBI protocol as their standard process for building interviews, creating consistent practice across the organization.

There is no comparison between a two-hour-long interview that includes evidences, performance tasks and questions and a 40-minute interview that limits discovery to a list of predetermined questions. The value of the screening process is that it allocates time to the most important part of the interview—the face-to-face time spent with the very top candidates. Those candidates that experience the SBI consistently state that it was the best experience of their professional career, one that allowed them to truly showcase their skills and knowledge. The rigor of the SBI sets the tone for expectations once on the job and very clearly expresses the value the organization places upon hiring top talent.

Minutes	Activity
0 interview minutes 60 candidate minutes	**Screening Activity (one week or more before the interview)** Indicator—Evidence Domain—Classroom Environment As a part of the screening assignment (phase two in the screening process), you asked the candidate to submit a behavior management plan that clearly explains expectations for learning and achievement. This time does not count toward the total interview time but addresses one indicator and one domain of the SBI protocol, providing rich information to the interview team in advance of the face-to-face interview.
0 interview minutes 15 candidate minutes	**Writing Prompt** Indicator—Response Domain—Planning and Preparation Upon arrival, you ask your administrative assistant to provide the candidate with a question requiring a written response. The question presented a scenario requiring the candidate to use their knowledge of special education students. The candidate is provided a quiet space and 15 minutes to complete the writing prompt. Once the allotted time has expired, the candidate is brought into the interview room. Again, this time does not count toward the face-to-face interview time as the candidate is completing the exercise prior to meeting with the interview team.
10 minutes	**Interview and Introductions** The interview team welcomes the candidate and asks a very simple warm-up question to put the candidate at ease. "Tell us a little about yourself" is a typical warm-up question. Next, they explain that the interview will last approximately two hours and will be comprised of performance tasks and questions.
15 minutes	**Mock Parent Conference** Indicator—Performance Domain—Professional Responsibilities Ask the candidate to participate in a mock parent conference, during which an interview team member plays the role of an irate parent. Debrief afterwards, always asking the candidate what she/he would do differently, given the opportunity.

Figure 3.3 Sample Standards-Based Interview schedule

15 minutes	**Student Assessment** Indicator—Evidence Domain—Planning and Preparation In your invitation to interview, you informed the candidate that they should bring with them a student learning assessment that demonstrates congruence with instructional outcomes. During this portion of the interview, ask the candidate to share their artifact and explain how the assessment aligns with instructional outcomes. Interview team members should ask probing questions that reveal the candidate's design thinking.
35 minutes	**Mini-Lesson** Indicator—Performance Domain—Instruction In your invitation to interview, you informed the candidate that they would be teaching a 20-minute mini-lesson to a small group of students and the interview team. Provide the candidate with five minutes to set up for their lesson, 20 minutes to teach the lesson and use the final 10 minutes to debrief the lesson with the candidate, again asking the candidate what she/he would do differently given the opportunity.
30 minutes	**Traditional Questioning** Indictor—Response Domains—Classroom Environment, Instruction, Professional Responsibilities Set 1 (2–3 questions)—Ask the candidate questions about how they would respond to various classroom management scenarios (pre-plan your scenarios). Set 2 (2–3 questions)—Ask the candidate questions about how they use questioning and discussion techniques to elicit student learning. Set 3 (2–3 questions)—Ask the candidate questions about participating in a school and district projects, trainings and initiatives.
15 minutes	**Conclusion** During the last 15 minutes of the two-hour interview, the team can ask follow-up questions about any parts of the interview, including the pre-screening and written assignments. Additionally, this is an opportunity for the candidate to ask questions of the team. Conclude by thanking the candidate for engaging in what was a very interactive interview!
Total Time: 2 hours	**Total Protocol Hits** Indicators Addressed—Evidence (2), Performance (2), Response (4) Domains Addressed—Planning and Preparation (2), Classroom Environment (2), Instruction (2), Professional Responsibilities (2)

Figure 3.3 (Cont.)

Step 3 Make the Offer

Now that your interviews are complete, use your interview team to rank all face-to-face interviewed candidates and gain consensus on the top two candidates. In making a final selection, you always want to have a top choice and a backup candidate. A great candidate is likely to have other offers and you want to be prepared to hire your backup if needed. Before you extend an offer, reach out to the references of your top candidates. No matter who the candidate lists as references, always contact a current and former direct supervisor. Past performance is the strongest indicator of future performance making this information very valuable to you prior to extending an official offer. Everything checked out? Great. Make your offer! And, if it is refused, you do not have to start at the beginning. Your process has already identified strong backup candidates. Congratulations. You have used your time where it matters the most—selecting the best candidate for your vacancy.

 ## Action Steps for Hiring

With your Strategic Talent Leadership Team, identify next steps in becoming more strategic in your hiring practices.

- Which best practices are you already using to successfully hire talent?
- Which new practices would you like to begin implementing?
- In Table 3.2, list new practices for implementation, data/resources needed, a lead team member and the timeline for putting your next steps into action.

Table 3.2 Action Steps for Hiring

Best Practice	Required Resources	Lead	Timeline

Talent Analytics for Hiring

You have now assessed your current practices and identified some action steps. Below are the talent analytics, found in the Strategic Talent Leadership Scorecard (Appendix C), that you can use to measure and track your progress toward being a strategic talent leader.

1. Number of standards-based interviews conducted per month by position

2. Number and percentages of vacant teacher positions filled by the end of the school year

3. Number and percentage of vacancies remaining on the first day of school

4. Candidates of color who pass the screening process and are recommended for hire compared to Caucasian candidates

5. Acceptance rate of job offers

Case Study Response

Now that you have learned more about best practices for hiring educators, what advice would you give to Principal Lloyd? Write your response in the space below:

_____

_____

_____

_____

_____

References

Danielson, Charlotte. (2009). *Implementing the framework for teaching in enhancing professional practice*. Alexandria, VA: ASCD.

Egalite, A. K. (2015). Representation in the classroom: The effect of own-race teachers on student achievement. *Economics of Education Review, 45*, pp. 44–52. Retrieved from https://www.sciencedirect.com/science/article/abs/pii/S0272775715000084

Holt, S. (2015). *The impact of teacher demographic representation on student attendance and suspensions.* IZA DP No. 9554. Retrieved from http://ftp.iza.org/dp9554.pdf

Konoske-Graf, A., Partelow, L., & Benner, M. (2016). To attract great teachers, school districts must improve their human capital systems. *The Center for American Progress.* Retrieved from: https://www.americanprogress.org/issues/education-k-12/reports/2016/12/22/295574/to-attract-great-teachers-school-districts-must-improve-their-human-capital-systems/

Lie, E. (2005). Hiring, Job Satisfaction, and the Fit Between New Teachers and Their Schools. *American Educational Research Association.* Montreal, QC: AERA.

LinkedIn. (2015). *Interesting facts about job interviews, job seeking and resumes.* Retrieved from: https://www.linkedin.com/pulse/interesting-facts-interviews-job-seeking-resumes-info-solutions/

Papay, J., & Kraft, M. (2016). The productivity costs of inefficient hiring practices: Evidence from late teacher hiring. *Journal of Public Policy and Management, 35*(4), pp. 791–817.

Rockoff, J. E., Jacob, B.A., Kane, T.J., & Staiger, D.O. (2008). Can You Recognize an Effective Teacher When You Recruit One? *National Bureau of Economic Research, Working Paper No. 14485.* Retrieved from: http://www.nber.org/papers/w14485.pdf

Spencer, L.M., & Spencer, S.M. (1993). *Competence at work - models for superior performance.* New York, NY: John Wiley & Sons.

Talent Acceleration

Assigning

It is August and White Oak Middle has a 7th-grade math vacancy on a depart-mentalized team of four teachers. The language arts and social studies teacher are going into their second years of teaching. The science teacher was just hired in January and is going to school at night to earn her teaching certifica-tion in order to clear an emergency license. The 6th- and 8th-grade teacher teams are very strong and Principal Martin does not want to risk disrupting them by moving teachers around, especially this close to the start of the school year. Reluctantly, he fills the 7th-grade math vacancy with the best candidate he could find—a recent college graduate with a degree in applied mathe-matics who is eligible for an emergency teaching license. Three weeks into the school year, his math teacher breaks down and quits.

Assigning Talent

Assigning is the practice of matching candidates with the role that is the best fit for the school's needs and the candidate's skill sets. The process of assigning teachers to roles impacts multiple factors such as performance, job satisfaction, retention and working conditions. A poor assignment can frustrate both the candidate and the supervisor, while a strong match can lead to enhanced candidate and team performance, ultimately benefitting students. It is for that reason that assigning a can-didate to the right role is a best practice in a strategic talent leadership approach.

Many principals confuse the process of placing and assigning can-didates. Placing is traditionally defined as the process of matching a candidate with as school, whereas assigning is strategically matching a candidate in a specific role, on a specific team and with specific students within a school (Behrstock & Coggshall, 2009). Both processes should be subject to considerations such as equitable distribution of talent across and within schools, demographic diversity and candidate potential for success based upon school and team culture.

Impacts of Assignment Patterns

Typical principal assignment behaviors consist of posting a vacancy notice, interviewing candidates for that specific vacancy, hiring the best candidate and filling the vacancy with that candidate. Because many factors feed into the front end of that process such as the number of candidates who apply, the quality of candidates who apply, the screening and hiring process used and the candidate's acceptance of job the offer, not all assignment patterns benefit students. In fact, teachers with little or no experience tend to be assigned to the classes with the lowest performing and lowest income students (Feng, 2010). In a national study of principal hiring and assigning behaviors, Donaldson (2013) found that when beginning teachers experienced more challenging job assignments, they resigned at significantly higher rates, resulting in principals having to begin the vacancy posting, candidate screening, interviewing and hiring process all over again. This pattern, when adopted as a common practice, will further disadvantage our most fragile students and only serve to widen the opportunity and achievement gap.

Principals who strategically assign candidates to vacancies pay attention to the alignment between candidate skill set and the vacancy. They assess their current faculty talent strengths and make necessary internal job assignment shifts first, creating the ideal vacancy to best leverage the skills and knowledge of the newly hired candidate. Strategic talent leaders assign new and less experienced teachers more equitably (Loeb, Beteille, & Kalogrides, 2012), to the advantage of both the teacher and students. In the long term, a greater investment of time and care in making strong job assignments will lead to higher retention rates, job satisfaction and improved student outcomes (Center for Education Policy Research, 2015). All of these will result in school leaders spending more of their time on

Table 4.1 Strategic Talent Leadership Insights for Assigning

Strategic Practice	Yes	Not Yet
Our organization strives to achieve congruence of demographics between educators and students at each school.		
Our organization uses site-based educator talent maps to achieve equitable student access to talent across and within schools.		
Our organization ensures that first-year teachers are not assigned more than two course preparations per semester.		
Our organization monitors transfers in and out of schools by number of teachers and effectiveness level with particular attention paid to highly impacted schools.		
Our organization avoids making surplus placements into highly impacted schools.		

making forward progress and less remaining in a continuous state of hiring for vacancies.

Strategic Talent Leadership Insights for Assigning

With your Strategic Talent Leadership Team, review the strategic talent leadership practices for assigning (see Table 4.1). If you are currently engaging in a practice, check 'yes.' If not, check 'not yet' and consider how this practice could be adopted by your organization as you read through the best practices described in this chapter.

Best Practices for Assigning Talent

Student and Staff Demographic Alignment

Forty percent of schools in the United States do not have a single teacher of color (National Collaborative on Diversity in the Teaching Force, 2004).

Yet, more than 50 percent of students in the United States identify with a racial minority group (National Center for Education Statistics, 2014). Numerous research studies have concluded that minority students benefit academically, are more likely to graduate and are more likely to enroll in a four-year college or university when they have been taught by at least one teacher of color (Egalite, Kisida, & Winters, 2015; Learning Policy Institute, 2018). While principals may not be able to mirror student and faculty demographics one-to-one, the addition of effective minority educators should be a priority goal. When making strategic assignments, school leaders should aim for every student, especially students of color, to have the opportunity to be assigned to a teacher of color at some point during their student career. As referenced in Chapter 2—Recruiting, this can be accomplished by sourcing more educators of racial minority identity and establishing recruiting partnerships with Historically Black Colleges and Universities (HBCUs) and Hispanic Association of Colleges and Universities (HACUs).

Equitable Distribution of Talent

In addition to prioritizing student access to educators of color, strategic principals ensure equitable access to effective educators both across and within schools. "No matter how you 'define' teacher effectiveness, low-income, minority and lower achieving students end up with the least effective teachers" (Goldhaber, Lavery, & Theobald, 2015). Achieving equity across and within schools can be measured by looking at key indicators described in Table 4.2. When strategic leaders track the distribution of teachers, by effectiveness indicator, across and within schools, patterns may reveal the causes of inequitable access, which lead to the widening of the opportunity and achievement gap (Darling-Hammond, 1995; Kain & Singleton, 1996; Lankford, Loeb, & Wyckoff, 2002; Presley, White, & Gong, 2005; Shields et al., 1999). Examining equity data can aid in ameliorating hidden inequities.

In addition to analyzing data, the practice of more equitable distribution can be accomplished in several very tangible ways:

- Monitoring and regulating the new hire placement of teachers into schools at the district level to achieve the desired distribution.

Table 4.2 Equitable Access to Effective Educators across and within Schools

Equitable Access across Schools	Equitable Access within Schools
– The percentage of highly effective teachers by school type (high-need vs average-need)	– Teacher effectiveness levels by student demographics (race, SES, ESOL, achievement level)
– Preservice quality indicators (GPA, Praxis, ACT, SAT) by school type	– Teacher years of experience by student demographics
– Gender and racial diversity of teachers by school type	– Teacher certification by student demographics
– Teacher years of experience distribution by school type	– Teacher advanced certification and degrees by student demographics
– Alternatively licensed teacher distribution by school type	– Teacher attendance by student demographics
– Teacher National Board Certification and Advanced Degree achievement distribution by school type	– Teacher effectiveness level by course assignment (regular vs advanced courses)
– Retention rates of teachers by school type	– Student assignment to courses by student demographics
– Principal effectiveness rating by school type	– Student class size by student demographic

- Monitoring and regulating interschool transfers such that no one school is a significant gainer or loser of talent.

- Avoiding the placement of surplus teachers into highly impacted schools, especially if surpluses are decided by seniority.

- Hand-scheduling students into classes based upon the student's achievement and growth levels in alignment with the teacher's academic impact results.

- Ensuring that students who are not yet on grade level and/or who are not yet making expected growth are not assigned to a below average teacher more than one year in a row (Sanders & Rivers, 1996).

- Offering incentives to highly effective teachers to encourage self-selection into highly impacted schools.

Local school board policies and state laws will sometimes determine which of these practices principals can leverage to achieve an ideal distribution. In order to ultimately close the achievement gap, the most effective teachers would be assigned to the most fragile students. While controversial, this practice would ensure equitable outcomes for all students.

Limit Course Preparations for Beginning Teachers

An important consideration in making a strong assignment for beginning teachers is work load. Beginning teachers are often managing multiple life changes at once—finishing college, starting a new job, moving to a new location, moving into their first apartment or house, etc. The transition from full-time student to full-time teacher can be jarring. In order to ease this transition, principals wishing to nurture, develop and retain new talent should attempt to mitigate unnecessary barriers to success. One way to do this is limiting the number of course preparations for beginning teachers. We once supported a brand new teacher, working on an emergency license, who was assigned four different course preparations per semester *and* was split between two schools. She was asked to use her lunch break to transport herself between buildings. Not surprisingly, she began thinking about resigning before the end of her very first semester. With additional support from her educator preparation program coach, she was able to make it to the end of the school year and found a job within the same district that allowed her to work at a single school, full time. She was amazed at how easy teaching was her second year. But, her first year should not have been so difficult. If her principal had been able to limit her course preparations to two, and rework the schedule to keep her in the building full time (he opted for two half-time teachers vs one full-time), this brand new teacher's first year would have been much less stressful. While this may be easier to accomplish in middle and high schools, elementary principals can use departmentalization to limit course preparations for their teachers. By reducing the workload of first-year teachers through limited course preparations, placing caps on 'extra duties as assigned,' and not requiring committee work, principals can provide beginning teachers with a strong start, resulting in a desire to return for a second year.

Limit Transfers In and Out of Schools

I started my first principalship midyear, during the month of the transfer window, with a strong faculty, many of whom had been at the school since it opened seven years earlier. In that time, the school had gone through five principals, the last of which was well-loved by the faculty. Unbeknownst to me, she had promised the most effective faculty that she would transfer them into her new school for the following school year. Before I knew it, almost 100 percent of my effective teachers had signed transfer paperwork to move with their current leader. Only three weeks into the new job, I was facing 14 vacancies in core teaching positions for the upcoming school year at one of the hardest-to-staff schools in the county.

As an emerging leader, I did everything I knew to recruit top talent into my school. I attended all of the job fairs, reviewed hundreds of applications, observed my current student teachers for potential hire and reached out to contacts across the county in an attempt to replace the talent that I was about to lose. To no avail, I was unable to secure any experienced teachers for my school. In a last ditch effort to provide my students with an effective education, I used my Title I dollars to create three instructional coaching positions to work with the 77 percent of my faculty that was classified as a beginning teacher (<3 years of experience). While our performance dropped, the strategy staved off a full-blown disaster and the school began to rebuild its student achievement muscle over the next few years with the extra provision of support.

This example is one of many in which leaders, wanting to provide the very best for their own students, can cause harm to others. By draining the metaphorical fuel from my gas tank, I had no way of reaching my destination. Monitoring transfers in and out of school by number and level of effectiveness could have allowed both my school and the former leader's new school access to highly effective educators. At the district level, tracking transfer data will enable organizations to better manage the placement of faculty across schools and assignment within them to the benefit of all students.

Avoid Surplus Placements without Input

Generally speaking, principals are good, honest people. That is, until surplus placement time rolls around! As soon as the 's' word is muttered, principals become fully staffed, have no retirements and are all of the sudden considering trading in position allocations for additional instructional funds. No one wants a surplus teacher dropped onto their faculty without input. Who can blame them? While the majority of surplus teachers are the least experienced, due to the last-hired-first-fired policies of many districts, these teachers are quite often energetic, eager and effective new teachers who do not deserve to be treated as if they are expendable (Levin, Mulhern, & Schunk, 2005).

Regardless, the process of selecting and hiring the right talent onto an existing team is essential. It is for that reason that surplus placements without input should be avoided, especially at highly impacted schools. As an alternative to forced placements, districts can surplus teachers into a pool and allow principals to interview and hire for a best match. If at the end of the hiring season surplus teachers remain unselected, the district can offer them nonteaching or substitute teaching opportunities as an alternative to a reduction in force (RIF). This allows principals to maintain the talent selection control for their schools and ensures strong matches will be made via mutual consent, resulting in longer-term retention and increased job satisfaction for the surplus teachers.

Talent Tool 4—Site-Based Talent Map

In our chapter case scenario, Principal Martin was doing his best to protect his 6th- and 8th-grade team members from having to move grade levels. A strategic leader would advocate for his/her students equitable access to highly effective teachers first and worry about faculty members' course assignment preferences as a secondary concern. In this case, the assignment of yet another inexperienced teacher onto an already weak team will not lead to maximum student achievement and success. Too often, principals fill vacated positions versus filling a position allocation. Just because a 7th-grade math position was vacated does not require that the principal hire a new 7th-grade math teacher. As a strategic leader, the principal should create a Site-Based Talent Map to assess the strengths of the entire faculty. Then, she/he should determine the best assignment of the vacancy compared to the available candidates.

By using a Site-Based Talent Map to make visible areas of strength and weakness in skills and knowledge levels, principals can ensure a strong distribution of teacher talent at each grade level and in each subject. The first step in creating your Site-Based Talent Map is to populate a matrix similar to the example in Table 4.3. In column one, list

Table 4.3 Site-Based Talent Map

Name	Classroom Management	Lesson Planning	Parent Engagement	Special Education	Content Knowledge
6th-Grade LA	X		X	X	X
6th-Grade MA	X	X	X		X
6th-Grade SCI		X	X		X
6th-Grade SS	X	X		X	
7th-Grade LA		X		X	X
7th-Grade MA	Current Vacancy				
7th-Grade SCI			X		X
7th-Grade SS	X			X	
8th-Grade LA		X	X		X
8th-Grade MA			X	X	X
8th-Grade SCI	X	X		X	X
8th-Grade SS	X		X	X	X
Math Candidate 1		X	X		X
Math Candidate 2	X			X	X

all of your allocated positions and the names of the teachers currently assigned to each role. Across row one, list the skills and knowledge that are important for success in your building. In this example, classroom management, lesson planning, parent engagement, knowledge of special education and content area knowledge were deemed the most important teacher attributes.

After identifying column and row headings, school leaders should work to identify which areas of knowledge and which skills are held by the actual teacher currently assigned to that position. Next, populate two additional rows with the knowledge and skills of the potential candidates for the position. Based upon the sample Site-Based Talent Map, would you put a newly hired candidate into the 7th-grade math vacancy? Or, would you transfer the 6th- or 8th-grade math teacher into the 7th-grade vacancy and assign the candidate to the position newly vacated by your internal transfer? Which candidate would you select and why?

Most principals who have examined this sample talent map would transfer the 6th-grade math teacher into the 7th-grade position, bringing the much needed strengths of classroom management, lesson planning and

Table 4.4 Action Steps for Assigning

Best Practice	Data/Resources	Lead	Timeline

parent engagement to the team. They would then hire Math Candidate 2 who has strong classroom management and knowledge of special education and place that candidate in the 6th-grade math position. While no one candidate has all skills and knowledge necessary as an individual, the strategic principal will seek balance by building strong teams whose talents complement each other.

Action Steps for Assigning

With your Talent Development Team, identify next steps in becoming more strategic in your assignment practices.

- Which best practices are you already using to successfully assign talent?
- Which new practices would you like to begin implementing?
- Table 4.4 lists new practices for implementation, data/resources needed, a lead team member and the timeline for putting your next steps into action.

Talent Analytics for Assigning

You have now assessed your current practices and identified some action steps. Following are the talent analytics, found in the Strategic Talent Leadership Scorecard (Appendix C), that you can use to measure and track your progress toward being a strategic talent leader.

1. Congruence of demographic diversity between educators and students

2. Low-performing teachers by school

3. Beginning teachers assigned more than two course preparations (elementary teachers excepted)

4. Transfers in and out of schools by number and teacher effectiveness level

5. Surplus educator placements by school

Case Study Response

Now that you have learned more about best practices for assigning educators, what advice would you give to Principal Martin? Write your response in the space below:

_____

_____

_____

_____

_____

References

Behrstock, E., & Coggshall, J. (2009). *Key issue: Teacher hiring, placement and assignment practices*. Washington, DC: National Comprehensive Center for Teaching Quality. Retrieved from: https://files.eric.ed.gov/fulltext/ED543675.pdf

Center for Education Policy Research. (2015). *Mathematics teacher placement patterns: Colorado integration project districts*. Harvard Strategic Data Project. Retrieved from: https://cepr.harvard.edu/files/cepr/files/sdp-diagnostic-key-findings-colorado-math-teacher-placement.pdf

Darling-Hammond, L. (1995). The role of teacher expertise and experience in students' opportunity to learn. In P. Brown (Ed.), *Strategies for linking school finance and students' opportunity to learn* (pp. 19–23). Washington, DC: National Governors Association.

Donaldson, M. L. (2013). Principals' approaches to cultivating teacher effectiveness: Constraints and opportunities in hiring, assigning, evaluating, and developing teachers. *Education Administration Quarterly, 49*, pp. 838–882. Retrieved from: https://journals.sagepub.com.libproxy.highpoint.edu/doi/pdf/10.1177/0013161X13485961

Egalite, A. J., Kisida, B., & Winters, M. A. (2015). Representation in the classroom: The effect of own-race teachers on student achievement. *Economics of Education Review, 45*, pp. 44–56. Retrieved from: https://www.sciencedirect.com/science/article/abs/pii/S0272775715000084?via%3Dihub

Feng, L. (2010). Hire today, gone tomorrow: New teacher classroom assignments and teacher mobility. *Education Finance and Policy, 5*(3), pp. 278–316.

Goldhaber, D., Lavery, L., & Theobald, R. (2015). Uneven playing field? Assessing the teacher quality gap between advantaged and disadvantaged students. *Educational Researcher, 44*(5), pp. 293–307. DOI: 10.3102/0013189X15592622

Kain, J. F., & Singleton, K. (1996, May/June). Equality of educational opportunity revisited. *New England Economic Review*, pp. 87–114.

Lankford, H., Loeb, S., & Wyckoff, J. (2002). Teaching sorting and the plight of urban schools: A descriptive analysis. *Educational Evaluation and Policy Analysis, 24*(1), pp. 37–62.

Learning Policy Institute. (2018). *Teachers of color: In high demand and short supply. What's needed to spur recruitment and retention?* Retrieved from: https://learningpolicyinstitute.org/press-release/teachers-color-high-demand-and-short-supply

Levin, J., Mulhern, J., & Schunk, J. (2005). *Unintended consequences: The case for reforming the staffing rules in urban teachers union contracts.* New York, NY: The New Teacher Project. Retrieved from: https://files.eric.ed.gov/fulltext/ED515654.pdf

Loeb, S., Beteille, T., & Kalogrides, D. (2012). Effective schools: Teacher hiring, assignment, development, and retention. *Education Finance and Policy, 7*(3), pp. 269–304.

National Center for Education Statistics. (2014). *Enrollment and percentage distribution of enrollment in public elementary and secondary schools, by race/ethnicity and region: Selected years, Fall 1995 through Fall 2024*. Retrieved from: https://nces.ed.gov/programs/digest/d14/tables/dt14_203.50.asp?current=yes

National Collaborative on Diversity in the Teaching Force. (2004). *Assessment of diversity in America's teaching force: A call to action*. Retrieved from: https://www.nea.org/assets/docs/HE/diversityreport.pdf

Presley, J., White, B., & Gong, Y. (2005). *Examining the distribution and impact of teacher quality in Illinois*. Edwardsville, IL: Illinois Education Research Council. Retrieved from: http://ierc.siue.edu/documents/Teacher%20Quality%20IERC%202005-2.pdf

Sanders, W. L., & Rivers, J. C. (1996). *Cumulative and residual effects of teachers on future student academic achievement*. Knoxville, YN: University of Tennessee Value-Added Research and Assessment Center.

Shields, P. M., Esch, C. E., Humphrey, D. C., Young, V. M., Gaston, M., & Hunt, H. (1999). *The status of the teaching profession: Research findings and policy recommendations*. Santa Cruz, CA: Center for the Future of Teaching and Learning.

Onboarding

Ms. Holcombe was hired to teach language arts at a highly impacted urban middle school. After not receiving any communications from the school or the district after being hired, she made a call and was told to show up the day before school started. Not knowing when the work day began, Ms. Holcombe played it safe and showed up at 7 am, promptly reporting to the office. No one was there. At 8:30, the principal walked in, looked at her and scolded, "Teacher workdays are from 8 to 4. You should have been in your classroom by now!" He turned to the secretary who had since walked into the office and instructed her to give Ms. Holcombe a key to her classroom. The secretary spotted a veteran teacher who was in the office checking her mailbox and asked her if she would take Ms. Holcombe down to her classroom. Begrudgingly, the veteran teacher walked her to room 321 and offered, "Good luck! You'll need it!" Still, nothing could take away the joy she had from starting her first teaching job. Ms. Holcombe proceeded to unlock her classroom door and walked into 200 dusty textbook boxes stacked high on top of her student desks. Open house was less than eight hours away.

Onboarding Talent

Onboarding is the practice of front-loading new hires with the skills, information and resources they need to reach maximum productivity in minimal time. A strong onboarding program will immediately increase employee engagement in the organization and help them acculturate to the district. By ensuring that new hires' needs are met upfront, the chances of them being successful and remaining with the organization increase.

Onboarding builds a strong foundation from which all other strategic talent leadership practices stem, making it a critical component of any talent leadership approach.

If you think you recognized the teacher name in the case scenario, your suspicions are correct. This was my onboarding experience! I was 21 years old and could not wait to have my very own classroom. I was going to be that 'favorite' teacher that every adult cited as the one that changed their life. What I was naively unprepared for was the lack of enthusiasm of those around me. Instead of welcoming a newbie into the fold, they had taken bets on how long I would last before resigning. And, they were very close to being correct. I didn't know where to park, the location of the supply closet, how to sign my students up for library time, where the teacher bathrooms were or even how to call in sick when I ended up with strep throat. By February of my first year, I was filling out a resignation form and planning on teaching for the Peace Corps in Tanzania the following year when another new teacher told me, "I hear it gets better. If you stay, I'll stay." It was through the bonds of the beginning teacher experience that I made it to my second year of teaching. In truth, it did get better—a lot better. But, the first year did not have to be so difficult. A strategic onboarding experience could have lessened my stress and anxiety, thereby yielding my students a much more effective teacher.

Benefits of Onboarding

Onboarding is the welcome mat to your school door. How new hires cross the threshold between the candidate and employee experience sets the tone for the working conditions in your building. A robust and well-planned welcome can lead to increased productivity, job satisfaction and, ultimately, employee retention. But, a nonexistent or poorly executed onboarding experience can lead to early resignations. Up to 20 percent of turnover occurs within the first six weeks of employment (Marino, 2016), due to a lack of clear understanding of expectations, access to resources and information. In a Harvard study, researchers found that employees in organizations that offered the longest onboarding programs reached full productivity 34 percent faster than the average timeline of eight months (Ferrazzi, 2015). In education, this is even more crucial because teacher productivity equates to improved outcomes for student. "With only one chance to get this crucial step right," wrote Glazerman et al. (2010), "it's an area that can't be ignored." A weak start to a new job can result in job dissatisfaction and premature resignation, which is destabilizing for both students and faculty. Every resignation requires that the principal begin a candidate search anew, spending hours of valuable time replacing a teacher that could have been retained through the provision of onboarding support. A time investment will be required—either on the front end in the form of onboarding or on the back end as a result of a resignation. Strategic talent leaders choose to invest their time in onboarding for long-term retention.

 ## Strategic Talent Leadership Insights for Onboarding

With your Strategic Talent Leadership Team, review the strategic talent leadership practices for onboarding (see Table 5.1). If you are currently engaging in a practice, check 'yes.' If not, check 'not yet' and consider how this practice could be adopted by your organization as you read through the best practices described in this chapter.

Table 5.1 Strategic Talent Leadership Insights for Onboarding

Strategic Practice	Yes	Not Yet
Our organization engages employees in pre-boarding experiences.		
Our organization offers a 90-day onboarding program to all employees regardless of hire date.		
Our organization offers up-boarding experiences to certified and classified employees who are being promoted.		
Our organization offers Employee Resource Groups to underrepresented populations.		
Our organization issues Quality-of-Hire surveys to supervisors upon completion of new hire 90-day onboarding programs.		

Best Practices for Onboarding Talent

Pre-Boarding

Start *before* they start. The employee onboarding process begins with the acceptance of a position and extends through the first 90 days. Prior to the first day of employment, pre-boarding activities can mitigate the inevitable 'buyer's remorse' that results from leaving the limitless possibilities of a job search behind to embracing the reality of committing to a single job. The goal of pre-boarding is to sustain employee excitement about joining your team and engage them in acquiring organizational knowledge, establishing relationships and becoming invested in your school's strategic goals. Think of this process as dropping proverbial bread crumbs that begin at job acceptance and lead to the first day on the job. These bread crumbs may come in the form of a welcome letter from the superintendent, an invitation to a district-hosted social event for new hires, email introductions to team members, the provision of a new hire checklist from the principal or even a meet and greet with current faculty. No matter the format or method, principals need to engage new hires in continuous (at least weekly), warm, communication to maintain the level of excitement and momentum.

Onboard Year-Round

In order to provide all new hires with an exceptional onboarding experience you will need to offer onboarding activities year-round. Most school districts only offer a beginning of the year, multiday, new employee orientation that is designed to successfully launch the school year. In your organization, this might look like bringing dozens, if not hundreds, of new teachers to a large conference space to hear a series of speakers, attend some breakout sessions and even network with district leaders. But, not all new employees are hired over the summer with a start date in August. Most districts hire year-round with the bulk of hires falling just before the start of the fall and spring semesters. Realistically, this can't be repeated all year long for every new hire. So how can you as a principal, with limited time, deliver an onboarding experience to every new hire? You maximize employee learning while minimizing your time investment.

As an alternative to duplicating multiday onboarding orientations throughout the year, transition the bulk of your content online and offer a reduced face-to-face experience. Develop, as a district, human resources (HR) team, or group of principals, a series of online learning modules that feature a welcome from the superintendent, an overview of district culture, district points of pride, introductions to the board of education and senior staff members, district policies and procedures, an overview of your strategic plan, school safety and OSHA required training, equity and inclusion and other relevant topics that should be reviewed prior to an employee's first day of work. The online format of the modules allows employees to review the content flexibly and at their own pace. Licensed employees may have one group of modules to complete, while non-licensed review only those relevant to their noninstructional duties, allowing for a more personalized experience. Because the modules are available online, they will require no time investment from principals or HR staff beyond the initial investment in developing the online content.

Shifting content online will allow you to offer a face-to-face experience that is significantly shortened from multiple days to one or two hours, during which legal paperwork, benefits registration and compliance tasks can be completed. This should be completed prior to the new employee's start date but, because of the reduced time, the face-to-face session can be offered two or three times a month throughout the school year by members of your HR team. Shifting from a one-and-done new employee orientation that is only offered in August to an online format followed by a short face-to-face session provides all new employees with an onboarding experience no matter when they are hired.

Up-Boarding

New employees are not the only ones that need strong onboarding experiences. Too often, team members are promoted from within an organization, tasked with an increased scope of duties and influence, without being provided any transitional training and support to ensure their success. While some promotions, such as teacher assistant to teacher, or teacher to principal, require formal training and licensure, many others do not. School districts are infamous for promoting from within, taking a principal and naming them director, taking a director and moving them up to executive director, and so forth, assuming that success in the current role will guarantee success in a higher level role. And, while past performance is the best predictor of future success (Ouellette & Wood, 1998), it is insufficient preparation for accelerating productivity in a new role. No matter the tenure of the employee, a new role should be coupled with an onboarding experience. A 2016 study by the Human Capital Institute found that "81% [of employers] agree onboarding internal hires is equally as important as onboarding external hires, but only 27% report they effectively onboard employees that are promoted or moved to a new position." In the case of internal promotions, we differentiate up-boarding from onboarding. Current employees do not need to be onboarded into the organization, rather, their success depends upon being up-boarded into a promoted role. This includes but is not limited to—(a) a deep understanding of the knowledge and skills required for success in the role, (b) behavioral expectations of the employee in the new role, (c) the provision of resources (budget, technology, personnel), (d) a discussion of success metrics and (e) leadership training in support of the level of supervisory duties and influence. Just as with onboarding, up-boarding practices accelerate productivity, increase job satisfaction and, therefore, lead to increased retention. Employees who experience strong onboarding and up-boarding supports are 50 percent more likely to remain working in their organization (Paradigm Learning, 2019).

Employee Resource Groups

Underutilized in education, Employee Resource Groups (ERGs), originally referred to as affinity groups back in the 1960s, are an excellent onboarding enhancement strategy for connecting new and existing employees to other team members with similar experiences or interests. Employees who develop strong social networks and workplace friendships report greater job satisfaction and demonstrate lower rates of attrition (Winstead, Derlega, Montgomery, & Pilkington, 1995; Paradigm Learning, 2015), which is crucial during the very first years of teaching. Principals and districts who do not currently leverage ERGs are potentially missing out on opportunities to achieve improved working conditions, increased employee retention, improved organizational culture and an external reputation for being a preferred workplace.

Launching an ERG, or multiple, is not difficult. As a principal or district leader, your primary role in getting an ERG started is twofold—first, communicate that your ERG exists and second, provide opportunities for the group to meet. You might start by forming an ERG for first-year teachers. Networking opportunities can be scheduled throughout the year and vary in location and purpose. The first meeting could be a new teacher social hosted at a local restaurant followed, the next month, by an informal solution sharing session at a coffee house. ERG meetings can also include professional development. For new teachers, hosting a guest speaker who shares strategies for involving parents or creating standards-based formative assessments might be shared topics of interest. The purpose of ERG gatherings can range from networking, socializing, resource sharing, problem-solving to learning. The purpose is to provide resources, in many forms, to like-minded groups. Commonly found ERGs across all professions include groups that share a common gender, race, sexual orientation, language or other protected class. Within education, groups that share a common interest based upon grade level or subject area taught, career interests (emerging leaders) or job duties may be popular. Pairing ERGs with the onboarding process further expedites employee productivity, engagement and the relationships that serve to keep educators in the profession and in your school.

Evaluate the Quality of Hire

Onboarding should always conclude with an evaluation of the quality of hire. An Aptitude Research Partners study found that when organizations invest the time in evaluating the quality of the personnel hired, they are three times as likely to experience an increase in retention rate and performance compared to organizations that do not (McIlvaine, 2019). This evaluation need not be extensive or difficult. It can be done by issuing two separate surveys—one to the newly hired employee and one to the hiring principal.

The employee evaluation of the onboarding process can be a simple online survey that is activated by the HR office after the first 90 days. The survey should ask employees to evaluate the onboarding experience and provide feedback about what information, training and resources are still needed in order that they feel prepared for success. It is important to not only ask Likert-style questions that can be quantitatively analyzed but also capture qualitative, open-ended feedback by asking questions like:

- How strong is the match between you and your mentor? Have you been assigned the right person to position you for future success?
- Do you fully understand the expectations of you in this new role?
- To what extent does your job align with what you were led to believe?
- Now that you have been in your role for 90 days, are there areas in which you would like additional support?
- To what degree have you established professional relationships with your coworkers?
- Are there ERGs with which you would like to be connected?
- To what extent did our onboarding process help you to feel included in the organization?
- What can we do to better ensure your success in this role?

The results of this survey will not only inform principals about needed support but also provide rich information for continuous improvement resulting in the increased effectiveness of the entire onboarding process for future new hires.

The audience for the second survey, to be sent at the same 90-day mark, should be the hiring principal. In this survey, you should attempt to capture the effectiveness of the recruiting and hiring process as well as the quality of the hire itself, again using both Likert-style questions and a variety of open-ended questions. Questions to consider including are as follows:

- To what degree do you feel that the screening process was effective in identifying a highly effective teacher (or other role)?

- To what degree do you feel that the district provided onboarding experiences prepared your new hire for success?
- How long after the initial hire do you feel it took the new hire to become effective?
- Are there any areas of support that you feel the district could have provided to the new hire prior to their start date?
- Would you hire this person again?
- Would you hire this person again for the same role?
- Do you anticipate recommending that the new teacher return to your school next year?
- Do you anticipate that the new teacher will want to return to your school next year?

Survey results from newly hired employees should be shared with the hiring principal and results from the hiring principal survey should be shared with the HR department. Surveys should never be issued unless there is a commitment to taking action on the results by incorporating the findings into a continuous improvement cycle. Using this data, the entire onboarding process should be revised and strengthened annually. A robust and thoughtful onboarding experience will increase employee job satisfaction, retention, performance and working conditions. These, in turn, will help to grow your team of talented educators who are well able to positively impact student outcomes.

Strategic Talent Leadership Tool 5— 90-Day Site-Based Onboarding Plan

While working in a district that hired over 800 new employees per year, I led a team that devised a four-phase onboarding process. The first phase was activated upon acceptance of the job offer and included the delivery of online onboarding modules, as described earlier in this chapter. Phase two was the face-to-face new employee orientation meeting during which all paperwork was signed and compliance tasks completed. The next step of the process represented a transition of activity from the district level to the school site where the principal, or supervisor, used Strategic Talent Leadership Tool 5, the 90-Day Site-Based Onboarding Plan, to lead a fully customizable onsite system of support. At the completion of this 90-day plan, phase four, the onboarding evaluation survey was issued to both the new employee and principal.

Strategic Talent Leadership Tool 5, the 90-Day Site-Based Onboarding Plan, represents a support system that would have prevented the challenges described in this chapter's case scenario. When principals embrace the importance of providing well-planned, intensive support during the onboarding period, stressors such as those I experienced during my first year of teacher can be lessened if not eliminated altogether. The first step in implementing the 90-Day Site-Based Onboarding Plan is to gain the commitment of your school leadership and/or district to engage in the process. Ideally, your school leadership team or district HR advisory team would have a discussion about what supports should be included in a 90-day site-based onboarding experience. A primary source of information for this discussion is your most recent group of new hires. Having just experienced the recruiting, hiring and assigning procedures in your district, they are primed for letting you know what should be included in their onboarding process.

As a result of this discussion, team members should brainstorm all content, resources and supports that should be a part of the 90-day onboarding. This can be facilitated by writing ideas on chart paper, a white board or my favorite method—one idea per Post-It Note. Individual Post-It Notes can then be moved around, in sequence, to create the 90-day process from start to finish. Finally, populate a checklist to create the formal 90-Day Site-Based Onboarding Plan and share it with all principals or school leaders in your district for use in onboarding new teachers. Over time, this same process can be used to develop an onboarding experience for all roles in your district. Figure 5.1 is a sample 90-day plan that can be adapted for use in your own school or district for new teacher onboarding. The plan assumes that a district level onboarding has already occurred.

At the district level, an HR advisory team can be formed and leveraged to develop a standardized 90-Day Site-Based Onboarding Plan that can be customized at the school level for new teachers, certified support roles and noncertified staff. Ideally, this 90-day plan would be developed for each role within the district, ensuring that 100 percent of employees had

90-Day Site-Based Onboarding Plan			

Instructions: Each employee should be provided a 90-day site-based onboarding. This form should be used to track completion of onboarding activities. After each time segment, both the supervisor and new employee should initial to signify completion of all activities. At the end of the 90-day onboarding period, this completed form should be sent to your school's HR partner for inclusion in the new employee's file.

Employee	
Job Role	
Location	
Principal	
Start Date	
90th Day	

Timeline	Content/Activity	Principal Initials	Employee Initials
First Day	Welcome meeting with the principal		
	Parking space/area assigned		
	Mailbox assigned		
	Room key provided		
	Classroom assigned		
	Bathroom locations shared		
	Teacher workroom location shared		
	Procedures for accessing supplied shared		
	Procedures for making copies shared		
	Tour of facility and work area		
	Introduction to teammates and colleagues		
	Work hours and daily schedule reviewed		
	Class and student assignments shared		
	Lunch procedures and schedule shared		
	Review of emergency procedures shared		
	Lunch with a colleague		
First Week	Daily check-in with principal or designee		
	Mentor assigned		
	Organizational structure and leadership reviewed		
	School policies and procedures reviewed		
	Discussion of 'unwritten rules'		
	Procedures for taking leave reviewed		
	Job description and expectations reviewed		
	Curriculum resources shared (curriculum standards, pacing guides, lesson plans, formative and summative assessments, etc.)		
	Lesson planning procedures/expectations reviewed		

Figure 5.1 90-Day Site-Based Onboarding Plan

	Technology access provided (email account, gradebook, student attendance, website, curriculum portal, benefits portal, etc.)		
	Lunch with mentor		
Second Week	Daily check-in with principal or designee		
	Review of employee evaluation instrument and timeline		
	Individual Education Plan's (IEP) reviewed and procedures explained		
	Review student cumulative folders		
	Parent engagement and communications expectations reviewed		
	Classroom and behavior management plans and expectations reviewed		
	Lesson plans reviewed for alignment to curriculum		
	Classroom check-in to ensure proper resources have been allocated		
First Month	Weekly check-in with principal or designee		
	Weather-related emergency procedures reviewed		
	Classroom and behavior management plan reviewed		
	Lesson plans reviewed for alignment to curriculum		
	Check to ensure a strong mentor match and that mentor support is being provided regularly		
	Lunch with principal		
Second Month	Weekly check-in with principal or designee		
	Professional growth opportunities within the organization shared		
	Check to ensure that mentor support is being provided regularly		
	Lunch with principal		
Third Month	Weekly check-in with principal or designee		
	Check to ensure that mentor support is being provided regularly		
	Lunch with principal		
90th Day	90-Day On-Site Onboarding Review		
	Monthly check-in with principal or designee to continue the entire first year		

Figure 5.1 (Cont.)

Table 5.2 Action Steps for Onboarding

Best Practice	Data/Resources	Lead	Timeline

the knowledge and resources necessary to be productive. At a minimum, a generic certified and noncertified plan could suffice until your organization has the opportunity to further customize.

Action Steps for Onboarding

With your Talent Development Team, identify next steps in becoming more strategic in your onboarding practices.

- Which best practices are you already using to successfully onboard talent?
- Which new practices would you like to begin implementing?
- Table 5.2 lists new practices for implementation, data/resources needed, a lead team member and the timeline for putting your next steps into action.

Talent Analytics for Onboarding

You have now assessed your current practices and identified some action steps. Below are the talent analytics, found in the Strategic Talent Leadership Scorecard (Appendix C), that you can use to measure and track your progress toward being a strategic talent leader.

1. New hires who were engaged in pre-boarding prior to their start date
2. New hires who completed the onboarding process within 90 days of start date
3. Promoted employees who were provided an up-boarding experience

4. Employees engaged in an ERG

5. Number of employees who would be rehired based upon results of the quality of hire survey

Case Study Response

Now that you have learned more about best practices for onboarding educators, what advice would you give to Ms. Holcombe's principal? Write your response in the space below:

_____

_____

_____

_____

_____

References

Ferrazzi, K. (2015). *Technology can save onboarding from itself.* Brighton, MA: Harvard Business Review. Retrieved from: https://hbr.org/2015/03/technology-can-save-onboarding-from-itself

Glazerman, S., Isenberg, E., Dolfin, S., Bleeker, M., Johnson, A., Grider, M., & Jacobus, M. (2010). *Impacts of comprehensive teacher induction: Results from a randomized controlled study. Executive Summary.* Washington, DC: Mathematica Policy Research. Retrieved from:: http://ies.ed.gov/ncee/pubs/20104027/pdf/20104028.pdf

Human Capital Institute. (2016). *Onboarding outcomes: Fulfill new hire expectations.* Retrieved from: http://learn.skillsoft.com/STS-Website-AR-HCI-Talent-Pulse-Download.html

Marino, C. (2016). *18 jaw-dropping onboarding stats you need to know.* Eden Prairie, MN: Click Boarding. Retrieved from: https://www.clickboarding.com/18-jaw-dropping-onboarding-stats-you-need-to-know/

McIlvaine, A. R. (2019) *Unlocking the quality of hire conundrum*. Human Resource Executive, July/August, p. 11.

Ouellette, J. A., & Wood, W. (1998). Habit and intention in everyday life: The multiple processes by which past behavior predicts future behavior. *Psychological Bulletin, 124*(1), pp. 54–74.

Paradigm Learning. (2019). *The onboarding experience*. Retrieved from: https://www2.paradigmlearning.com/onboarding_experience

Winstead, B. A., Derlega, V. J., Montgomery, M. J., & Pilkington, C. (1995). The quality of friendships at work and job satisfaction. *Journal of Social and Personal Relationships, 12*(2), pp. 199–215. Retrieved from: https://doi.org/10.1177/0265407595122003

Mentoring

Ray Johnson was excited to begin his first year of teaching as a 6th-grade math teacher at Bowie Middle School. The school had a wonderful reputation and low teacher turnover. The community was very involved and supportive of the school. Ray felt fortunate to have landed at Bowie MS and was looking forward to challenging his students to achieve their best. On the night of open house, Ray had the opportunity to meet with parents and inform them of his high expectations. He was not going to accept any late work, did not believe in makeup assignments, was going to give automatic zeros for assignments missing names and was not going to allow students to earn extra credit. He shared with parents that bathroom breaks were to be taken in-between classes and that no tardies would be tolerated in his classroom. At the end of the evening, Ray was sure that he had inspired confidence in his students' parents and that they each understood that he was serious about educating their children. Before the end of the first grading period, Ray's principal called a meeting with him to discuss parent complaints. The president of the PTA, the mother of one of Ray's students, had started a petition to have Ray fired. The parents were angry about Ray's lack of flexibility, strictness in the classroom and lack of communication about their students' performance. Ray was deflated. He had watched all of those movies about how tough love got results with students. Where had he gone wrong?

Mentoring Talent

Mentoring is the practice of providing sustained support to educators new to their roles, whether to a new teacher, a new principal or a newly promoted executive educator. The typical teacher mentoring process lasts between one and three years and uses a gradual release model that supports the employee in taking increased responsibility for their own growth and success. There is strong evidence that mentoring and induction programs increase educator effectiveness as measured by student outcomes (Ingersoll & Strong, 2011). Additionally, the intensity and length of mentoring and induction programs is directly correlated to educator performance and retention (Glazerman et al., 2010). It is for that reason that mentoring is a critical component of the strategic talent leadership framework.

Activated at the beginning of a new role, mentoring is the process of matching a novice with an expert who can help navigate the unknown challenges of the new role. Often used interchangeably with 'coaching,' mentoring is actually a distinct type of support. Coaching typically targets one skill at a time, is provided for a short length of time and can be facilitated by either a peer or expert. On the contrary, mentoring is a broader provision of support that is delivered over multiple months by an expert. The goal of mentoring is to suppress roadblocks and barriers, such as those experienced by Ray Johnson in our case study, to gain maximum momentum within the first months and to sustain that growth over time.

Impacts of Mentoring on Student Achievement

Many studies have examined the impact of mentoring on student achievement. Generally speaking, school leaders are seeking confirmation that their investment in mentoring pays off in improved student outcomes. A study of teachers supported through The New Teacher Center's induction model reported a 22 percent return in the initial investment in the form of teacher retention (The New Teacher Center, 2019).

Yet, isolating the impact of a single intervention on student outcomes is challenging in that beginning teachers need and receive so many different forms of support from teacher peers, informal buddies, teacher leaders, administrators, university supervisors, friends and even family. In the most comprehensive meta-analysis of research on mentoring, Ingersoll and

Strong (2012) identified three trends across the impacts of mentoring on beginning teachers:

- Teacher commitment and retention
- Teacher classroom instructional practices
- Student achievement

Positive outcomes included higher job satisfaction of mentored teachers compared to those who did not receive mentoring and, as expected, higher retention rates. When teachers are happy in their roles, they are more likely to persist despite challenges. These same mentor-supported teachers tended to leverage more effective pedagogical strategies such as effective questioning, maintaining student time on task and strong classroom management strategies. As a result, there were some positive academic impacts achieved.

One of the studies included in the meta-analysis, a 2010 randomized control study conducted by Mathematica (Glazerman et al., 2010), found mixed reviews on impacts to teacher practices. However, the study did find that after three years, there were statistically significant differences in student achievement between those that did and did not receive mentoring. Students of those that received the more extensive mentoring increased, on average, 4 percentiles in reading and 8 percentiles in math. A more recent study by SRI International (2018) examined the impacts of the New Teacher Center's comprehensive induction program in several urban school districts across the county. What they found was that teachers who were immersed in the New Teacher Center's induction program, which included the provision of a trained mentor, were able to "increase student learning in grades 4–8 by an additional 2–4 months in ELA/reading and an additional 2–5 months in math." Education leaders who are allocating resources in support of beginning teacher mentoring should strongly consider these academic impacts as a part of their overall talent strategy.

Impacts of Mentoring on Teacher Retention

In addition to student achievement impacts, mentoring can play a significant role in beginning teacher retention. Behrstock-Sherratt, et al., at American Institutes for Research (2014) surveyed national and state teachers of the year to determine if there were any differentiators that helped them to be successful early in their careers. The top-cited provision of support leading to future effectiveness was access to a mentor. Yet, only 55 percent of those surveyed reported having a mentor. Other provisions of support-cited included supportive principals and strong placements within schools among others. These early provisions of support not only helped to retain these teachers, but were the foundation of careers that led to achieving the titles of state and national teacher of the year.

Similarly, a longitudinal study that began with a cohort of teachers starting their first year of teaching in 2007 found positive impacts of mentoring on retention (Gray, Taie, National Center for Education Statistics (ED), & Westat, Inc., 2015). As the cohort moved through their first five years of teaching, those with mentors were retained at higher rates than those teachers that did not—92 versus 84 percent after the first year, 91 versus 77 percent after the second year, 88 versus 73 percent after the third year and 86 versus 71 percent after the fourth. Additional studies found that not only were teachers with access to mentor support less likely to leave the profession, they were less likely than their counterparts to migrate to another school (Ronfeldt & McQueen, 2017). With attrition replacement costs estimated between 50 and 60 percent of an employee's salary (Tarallo, 2018), schools and districts cannot afford to lose teachers. Small investments in mentor training and additional compensation for mentor teachers could stave off high beginning teacher attrition and provide greater stability among faculty, resulting in improved outcomes for students.

Strategic Talent Leadership Insights for Mentoring

With your Strategic Talent Leadership Team, review the strategic talent leadership practices for mentoring (see Table 6.1). If you are currently engaging in a practice, check 'yes.' If not, check 'not yet' and consider how this practice could be adopted by your organization as you read through the best practices described in this chapter.

Table 6.1 Strategic Talent Leadership Insights for Mentoring

Strategic Practice	Yes	Not Yet
Our organization prepares and supports a carefully selected group of mentors who have a history of achieving positive student outcomes.		
Our organization ensures that all beginning teachers receive 90 minutes of mentor support each week for their first three years.		
Our organization ensures that all beginning teachers have opportunities to observe multiple master teachers.		
Our organization ensures that all beginning teachers use video recordings of themselves to reflect upon their practice.		
Our organization tracks beginning teacher progress using a Skills Mastery Checklist.		

Best Practices for Mentoring Talent

Training and Supporting Mentors

The first step in creating a robust mentoring and induction program for beginning teachers is to select and train a cadre of highly qualified master teachers with a history of positive student outcomes results. Effective mentors must, themselves, be coachable, willing to seek and receive feedback about their own practice in order to understand the perspective of the teachers they will mentor. They must not only be excellent at working with students, they must have a deep understanding of adult learners and their high need for relevance, timeliness, acknowledgment of prior knowledge and flexibility. Building a cadre of mentors requires taking into consideration multiple personnel characteristics:

- Years of experience and/or maturity
- Current and past performance
- Coachability
- Trustworthiness

- Ability to foster strong relationships
- Confidentiality
- Persistence in reaching goals
- Commitment to spending 90 minutes per week with each mentee

Once selected for their potential for success in supporting beginning teachers, mentors must be provided with substantial training in the skills and behaviors that must be modeled, practiced and mastered by beginning teachers. While fewer than 20 percent of districts have formal mentoring and induction programs (Konoske-Graf, Partelow, & Benner, 2016), many that do require mentors to be trained in supporting beginning teachers. There are formal mentor training programs offered by organizations such as the New Teacher Center, ETS and TNTP, as well as district-developed training programs that address confidentiality, relationship building, coaching stances, progress monitoring and other mentoring skills. In addition to initial mentor training, it is recommended that mentors are provided with:

- A venue for problem-solving, sharing resources and best practices with other mentors on a regular basis (either in person or online).
- Additional training to support beginning teachers in implementing special initiatives within school districts.
- Annual evaluations or feedback from mentees on the quality and effectiveness of their provided support services.
- 'Rust-removal' for mentors whose initial training is outdated.

Whether offered at the school or district level, your cadre of mentors should represent your most effective teachers. As such, recognizing their efforts through additional pay, release time, or through public promotion of their work is crucial in retaining them in these important roles.

Sustaining Levels of Mentor Support

In addition to building a cadre of mentors, strategic talent leaders will ensure that mentors are able to provide sustained levels of support to beginning teachers. Policy recommendations from the New Teacher Center include providing 90 minutes of mentor support each week for the first three years of a beginning teacher's career (Goldrick, 2016). For this to happen, school administrators must ensure an appropriate number of trained mentors, preferably in the same building as the mentee, for the number of beginning teachers to be supported. Upon hire, beginning teachers should be assigned a mentor that is a strong match for the mentee. This process is more art than science and can include factors as simple as having the same licensure area or role to having common preferences about whether to meet before or after school. By asking mentors and mentees a few questions about their preferred partner, school administrators can ensure viable matches. Once mentors and mentees are paired up, strategic talent leaders will ensure clear expectations of each role. These will vary and can include expectations such as:

- The day and time of the week when mentors and mentees should meet
- The length of weekly support
- The type of support provided
- Goal setting and progress monitoring
- Tracking of meetings and supports provided
- Making a strong match with a mentor teacher/master teacher

Many districts have found that using mentor/mentee logs are a good way of tracking the types support provided, the frequency of that support and the total time spent supporting beginning teachers. For districts that are required to report this data to their state and federal government funders, the more formal the tracking of the data, the better.

Structured Observations of Others

The first months of teaching represent a steep learning curve for most beginning teachers as they realize the challenges of planning five or more hours of instruction per day to meet the individual needs of dozens of students, assessing student learning, communicating with families, fulfilling their nonteaching professional duties within the school and preserving enough energy to maintain a personal life. In educator preparation programs, preservice teachers learn pedagogical strategies in a university classroom, outside the context of a K-12 school. Once in their student teaching internships, they may have practiced their skills in one or two different classroom settings. But, these were temporary and often not full-time teaching commitments. Once licensed and hired, beginning teachers face the reality of fully implementing what they learned in their preparation program, in a new school setting, with limited support. This experience has often been described by beginning educators as feeling like an egg nestled in a crate with 11 other teachers. All dozen eggs are in the same container but are isolated from each other in the same way classrooms separate teachers within a school. The best way to reduce the feeling of isolation and make practice public is to provide beginning teachers with multiple opportunities to observe other teachers.

Mentor teachers and administrators should identify master teachers throughout the building who exemplify best practices in a variety of areas such as classroom management, questioning techniques, formative assessment and student engagement. These master teachers may or may not also serve as mentors—they need only agree to have an open door policy that welcomes beginning teachers who want to observe their practice. This can be done during the beginning teacher's planning time, lunch time, or through providing coverage of teaching duties. Ideally, these observations are done with the beginning teacher's mentor and include:

- a pre-observation discussion to set the purpose of the observation;
- a post-observation to debrief and discuss what was dually observed by the mentor and mentee;
- opportunities to ask questions about the practices observed;
- goal setting as a follow-up to the observation; and,
- the option to conduct additional observations.

It is not recommended to observe master teachers with a checklist or observation protocol, rather, to go in and 'just be.' Allowing a beginning teacher the gift of watching, listening and feeling what it is like to be in the classroom of a master teacher without the distraction of tick boxes or forms provides them the most naturalistic opportunity to learn.

Ideally, beginning teachers would observe multiple teachers over the course of a school year.

Reflective Practice with Video

In working with both experienced and beginning teachers alike, one of the most illuminating practices is the use of video to capture and reflect upon teaching practice. I've watched veteran teachers as they have viewed themselves on film gasp, "I had no idea I did that!" Video keeps us honest—it doesn't allow us to hold onto the beliefs about how we teach. It forces us to confront the reality of how we teach. And, it is a revelation available to any teacher with access to a smart phone or digital video camera. Paired with a small tripod or even a more advanced device such as a Swivl, both audio and video of teaching practice can easily be captured.

Recommendations for using video include setting a specific practice to capture such as clarity of instructions, transitions between activities, questioning techniques, classroom management, etc. Additionally, teachers capturing video should limit the length to 5–7 minutes. If the focus is on a singular behavior or pedagogical skill, there is no need to view and analyze 20–30 minutes of video. The teacher would be better served reflecting upon four 5-minute videos than one 20-minute video. And, the quality of these short videos is not as important as sitting down, mentor and mentee, viewing the footage and discussing the degree to which the practice employed by the beginning teacher was effective. These developmental discussions can lead to additional videotaping, requests to go and observe master teachers implementing the same strategy, strategy-targeted coaching and even professional development. Video gives, beginning teachers especially, the most authentic understanding of the impact of their practice upon students in the classroom. Teachers wanting to share video with others can easily do so by setting up a password protected YouTube channel, share via Google Drive, DropBox, or a multitude of other file sharing platforms. Those seeking to view the best practices of others and share their practice on a more formal platform can access fee-based services such as The Teaching Channel. Whether video is viewed only by the teacher, by mentor and mentee together, or shared broadly, the use of this technology to reflect upon teaching practices is invaluable.

Progress Monitoring

If our case study teacher, Ray Johnson had access to a trained mentor, observations of master teachers and the opportunity to view his practice on video, he may have realized that his well-intentioned practices were actually detrimental to his students' learning and his relationship with their families. Self-awareness of our practices is always enhanced by tracking our progression along a continuum. To that end, the use of reflective logs and progress monitoring are highly recommended for beginning teachers. If beginning teachers are meeting, as recommended, with their mentor each week, reflective logs can help to inform the discussions had during those sessions as well as the resulting goal setting. As a next step, mentors and mentees can set short-term goals for the following week (Figure 6.1).

Beginning teachers who work with mentors to set weekly goals observe a master teacher demonstrating the targeted practice, view video of their own practice, reflect upon the differences between the master teacher's practice and their own and follow it up with a progress monitoring meeting are on track for continuous improvement and eventual mastery of essential skills. Strategic Talent Leadership Tool 6—Essential Skills Mastery Checklist is one method of tracking the impact of multiple

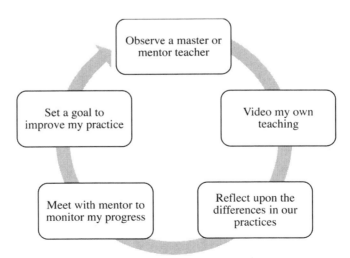

Figure 6.1 Sample Progress Monitoring Cycle

progress monitoring cycles throughout the first three years of a beginning teacher's career.

Talent Tool 6—Essential Skills Mastery Checklist

New to the profession, beginning teachers lack the perspective and wisdom of seasoned educators who have spent years learning the lessons of our profession. Through no fault of their own, they have yet to accumulate the quantity of experiences necessary to identify the skills most essential for early success. As master teachers, mentors have the task of helping their mentees to identify those experiences, make sense of them and translate them into skills that are known to lead to teaching effectiveness. The use of progress monitoring cycles is one way to control the pace at which those experiences are encountered and skills mastered. And, it helps to have a tool to systematically track these cycles. The Essential Skills Mastery Checklist is an easy way to identify, monitor and report out mentee progress.

The first step in creating an essential skills checklist is obvious—identify the skills deemed to be essential for success in your school. These can be generated by the mentor and mentee together, can be driven by the professional teaching standards, the evaluation instrument, or even taken from the research of master teachers who have developed models of essential skills such as Charlotte Danielson, James Stronge, Doug Lemov and so many others. Once those skills are identified, they should be used to populate the checklist. For each skill in the checklist, there is a space to document the observation of this skill as enacted by a master teacher (either modeled or observed authentically in the classroom), the reflection of the mentee watching him/herself implementing the skill on video and two spaces for the mentor to observe the skill implemented at the mastery level. Once all skills are deemed mastered, the mentor and mentee can then generate a set of more advanced skills, continuing to move the beginning teacher along a pathway from novice to experienced teacher. In Figure 6.2, ten of Doug Lemov's, *Teach Like a Champion (2015)*, techniques are used as sample skills. The mentor and mentee should ultimately decide upon the number of skills upon which to focus and the source of these skills.

ESSENTIAL SKILLS MASTERY CHECKLIST

For each identified skill, document the date when you:

☐ Observed a master teacher or mentor modeling the skill (MT)
☐ Used video to reflect upon your implemented practice of the skill (VR)
☐ Effectively implemented the skill on two separate occasions (1) (2)

Skill	MT	VR	1	2
1. Reject self-report	9/14	9/16	9/17	9/18
2. Targeted questioning	9/21	9/21	9/23	9/24
3. Standardize the format	9/28	9/30	10/1	10/5
4. Tracking, not watching				
5. Show me				
6. Affirmative checking				
7. Wait time				
8. Cold call				
9. Call and response				
10. Break it down				

Figure 6.2 Essential Skills Mastery Checklist

Action Steps for Mentoring

With your Talent Development Team, identify next steps in becoming more strategic in your mentoring practices.

- Which best practices are you already using to successfully mentor talent?
- Which new practices would you like to begin implementing?
- In Table 6.2, list new practices for implementation, data/resources needed, a lead team member and the timeline for putting your next steps into action.

Table 6.2 Action Steps for Onboarding

Best Practice	Data/Resources	Lead	Timeline

Talent Analytics for Mentoring

You have now assessed your current practices and identified some action steps. Below are the talent analytics, found in the Strategic Talent Leadership Scorecard (Appendix C), that you can use to measure and track your progress toward being a strategic talent leader.

1. Number of trained mentors available for assignment to mentees
2. Average minutes per week educators were provided support from a mentor during their first three years
3. The number of opportunities mentees have to observe master teachers
4. The number of opportunities mentees has to video and reflect upon their own teaching
5. The percentage of essential skills mastered by mentees by the end of their first, second and third years of teaching

Case Study Response

Now that you have learned more about best practices for mentoring educators, what advice would you give to Ray Johnson and his principal? Write your response in the space below:

_____

_____

_____

_____

_____

References

Behrstock-Sherratt, E., Bassett, K., Olson, D., Jacques, C., & Center on Great Teachers and Leaders at American Institutes for Research. (2014). *From good to great: Exemplary teachers share perspectives on increasing teacher effectiveness across the career continuum.* Washington, DC: Center on Great Teachers and Leaders.

Glazerman, S., Isenberg, E., Dolfin, S., Bleeker, M., Johnson, A., Grider, M., & Jacobus, M. (2010). *Impacts of comprehensive teacher induction: Final results from a randomized controlled study* (NCEE 2010-4027). Washington, DC: U.S. Department of Education.

Goldrick, L. (2016). *Support from the start—A 50-state review of policies on new educator induction and mentoring.* Santa Cruz, CA: The New Teacher Center.

Gray, L., Taie, S., National Center for Education Statistics (ED), & Westat, Inc. (2015). *Public school teacher attrition and mobility in the first five years: Results from the first through fifth waves of the 2007-08 beginning teacher longitudinal study.* First look (NCES 2015-337). Washington, DC: National Center for Education Statistics.

Ingersoll, R., & Strong, M. (2011). The impact of induction and mentoring programs for beginning teachers: A critical review of the research. *Review of Education Research, 81*(2), pp. 201–233.

Ingersoll, R., & Strong, M. (2012). What the research tells us about the impact of induction and mentoring programs for beginning teachers. *Yearbook of the National Society for the Study of Education, 111*(2), pp. 466–490.

Konoske-Graf, A., Partelow, L., & Benner, M. (2016). *To attract great teachers, school districts must improve their human capital systems.* Washington, DC: The Center for American Progress. Retrieved from https://www.americanprogress.org/issues/education-k-12/reports/2016/12/22/295574/to-attract-great-teachers-school-districts-must-improve-their-human-capital-systems/

Lemov, D. (2015). *Teach like a champion 2.0.* Hoboken, NJ: John Wiley & Sons.

Ronfeldt, M., & McQueen, K. (2017). Does new teacher induction really improve retention? *Journal of Teacher Education, 68*(4), pp. 394–410.

Schwartz, S. (2018). New teachers: "Evaluation of the new teacher center (NTC) i3 scale-up grant: Cohort 1 preliminary teacher and student impact." *Education Week*, *38*(7). Retrieved from https://www.edweek.org/ew/articles/2018/10/03/new-teachers-1.html

Tarallo, M. (2018, September 17). How to reduce employee turnover through robust retention strategies. Alexandria, VA: Society for Human Resource Management. Retrieved from https://www.shrm.org/resourcesandtools/hr-topics/talent-acquisition/pages/how-to-reduce-employee-turnover-through-robust-retention-strategies.aspx

The New Teacher Center. (2019). *Counting the cost: A commitment to educational equity that yields returns*. Santa Cruz, CA: The New Teacher Center.

DOMAIN III

Talent Advancement

- Training
- Coaching
- Evaluating

Talent Advancement

Training

Isabella Duarte is a 20-year veteran high school English teacher. Each year, she respectfully sits through the required OSHA courses, positive discipline training and workshops on the ever-changing annual focus. Two years ago, it was lesson study; last year featured reading across the curriculum; this year, the school is revisiting PLCs. Professional development in Duarte's school is haphazard, completed to meet district compliance requirements but never connected to strategic goals or her own professional growth. During the lunch break, she heard a rumor that a neighboring school district was starting a principal residency program for master teachers interested in moving into leadership roles. After lunch, Duarte tuned out the trainer and began filling out her online application for the Principal Residency Program in the other district.

Training Talent

Training is the practice of adding new skills and knowledge to an employee's current repertoire. It can be provided for the purpose of upskilling in preparation for taking on additional roles and responsibilities or for the purpose of increasing effectiveness in a current role. If at all possible, training should be personalized for each employee, recognizing their existing skills and knowledge and individualizing their professional growth pathway. When done well, this critical part of a strategic leadership approach will increase retention and effectiveness and provide a robust candidate pool for promotions.

But, providing well-planned and personalized training is not inexpensive. A recent study from TNTP estimated that nationally, school districts spend $18,000 per teacher each year on professional development (TNTP, 2015). That figure represents 37 percent of the annual average teacher salary in the United States. An investment of this size merits close examination, evaluation and attention from strategic talent leaders. Ten key questions for consideration by education leaders when making training decisions include:

1. What are the most common areas of weakness for teachers across my school or district and how does this align with the system of supports provided by the central office?

2. Does the professional growth my school offers align with teacher areas of weakness?

3. What are the triggers to activate additional support for educators?

4. For my teachers who are low performing, what supports are available to me that have helped teachers with similar challenges to improve?

5. Which of my teachers or instructional leaders are in need of advanced development in order to grow them into other leadership roles? What does this development look like?

6. Of the growth areas I have identified for my teachers, which ones are the biggest drivers of student improvement? And, how do I know?

7. What is the distribution of professional growth resources across the district (instructional coaches, conferences, training contracts, substitute costs)?

8. What formats of professional growth are being employed across the district?

9. Does the district calendar allow sufficient time for professional growth?

10. For the nonteaching days that are under my discretion, am I using that time for teacher professional growth and collaboration?

Additional considerations for leaders include the types of training and support that are provided. Personalizing learning experiences for adults requires that schools and districts think beyond the provision of traditional, face-to-face workshops and embrace authentic learning opportunities in many forms.

 # Types of Training

Adding new skills, knowledge and behaviors to an educator's repertoire is complex and ongoing. Authentic learning occurs at different times, in different contexts and through different delivery models for each educator (as it does for our students). Generally speaking, the most commonly found training activities can be classified into four groups (Table 7.1).

While each of these types of training is listed individually, the ideal approach to training would be to select all of the activities needed in order to fully address a desired learning outcome. An approach to building a personalized training experience will be addressed with Strategic Talent Leadership Tool 7, Training Wheels, later in the chapter.

Table 7.1 Four Types of Training Activities

Job Embedded Learning	Group and Collaborative Learning
Action research	Academies and cohorts
Apprenticeships	Book studies
Assessments	Conferences
Coaching	Co-teaching
Cross-training	Experiential learning activities
Inquiry cycles	Ignite sessions
Internships	Institutes
Job aids	Learning collaboratories
Job rotations	Lesson studies
Job shadowing	Networking lunches
Mentoring	Lunch-and-learns
Micro-learning	Open-space technology
Near peers	Professional learning communities
Reflective journaling	Seminars
Video-taping and reflection	Simulations
360° Feedback	Teach meets and ED camps
	Video feedback
	Workshops
	World Café

(*continued*)

Table 7.1 (Cont.)

Technology Facilitated Learning	Degree and Credential Earning Activities
Blended learning	Badges
Blogs	Certificates
Content curation	College and university degrees
Facebook groups and Facebook live	Credentials
Flipped classrooms	Endorsements
Gaming and SIMS	Licensure
Listservs	Micro-credentials
Online courses and MOOCS	Multi-tiered licensure
Pecha Kucha	
Personal learning networks	
Podcasts	
Twitter sessions	
Vines	
Virtual collaboration	
Wikis	

Are You Strategic about Training?

With your Strategic Talent Leadership Team, review the strategic talent leadership practices for training (see Table 7.2). If you are currently engaging in a practice, check 'yes.' If not, check 'not yet' and consider how this

Table 7.2 Strategic Talent Leadership Insights for Training

Strategic Practice	Yes	Not Yet
Our organization aligns all training to professional educator and evaluation standards.		
Our organization evaluates all training for impact on student outcomes.		
Our organization offers academies to prepare educators for future roles.		
Our organization supports educators in crafting individualized training experiences to achieve targeted goals.		
Our organization makes our training available to ancillary educators such as recruits, substitutes, student teachers and retirees.		

practice could be adopted by your organization as you read through the best practices described in this chapter.

Best Practices for Training Talent

Training is Aligned to Professional Teaching Standards and Evaluation Instruments

It may seem like common sense that as hiring managers and principals, we would use the same set of standards when we hire a teacher as when we train and evaluate them. However, that is not always the case. As described in Chapter 3, Hiring, screening and selection processes used by schools and districts do not always map back to professional teaching standards. Likewise, training and evaluating activities do not always draw their practice from professional teaching standards. Strategic talent leaders understand the importance of the alignment among all functions but especially these three. A logical chain of activity would be to hire the candidate that best exemplifies what we believe to be an effective teacher as described in the professional teaching standards used by our organization. During evaluation activities, we would use these same standards to determine current performance followed by the recommendation of training and support in the areas of weakness (Figure 7.1). If these three functions are well-aligned,

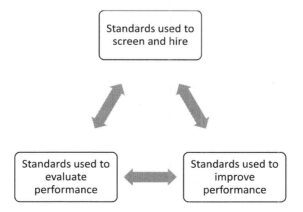

Figure 7.1 Alignment Among Hiring, Evaluating and Training Functions

it makes identifying and developing talent a much easier process for both the supervisor and the educator. It is the metaphorical equivalent to speaking the same language no matter the talent domain or function within which we are currently operating.

One way to ensure the alignment between training and professional teaching standards is to take all current training offered by your organization and map it to your standards. If it maps directly, you can then 'assign' educators to participate in training that correspond to their opportunities for growth. If it does not align, it will be important to ask the questions, 'Why are we offering this training?' 'How will this training improved student outcomes?' and 'How will we evaluate the benefits of this training to our faculty?' A sample of a training alignment map is provided below (Figure 7.2).

Once aligned, you can create a professional development catalogue, or searchable database, of training available to educators. This will make it easy to identify training by skill set and even easier to evaluate and report on impact.

Training is Evaluated for Impact

Evaluating the impact of training, especially in K-12 education is very difficult. Many factors drive teacher performance and student outcomes. It's nearly impossible, without conducting true randomized control research, to isolate the impact of a single provision of training to an educator. One of the best evaluation models I've used in determining the value of a training within education comes from Donald Kirkpatrick. In his book, *Evaluating*

Training	Professional Teaching Standards						
	1a	1b	1c	2a	2b	2c	3
Reading in the Content Areas					■		
Project Based Teaching and Learning							■
MTSS	■		■				
Effective Questioning Techniques				■	■		
Classroom Management	■						
Building Relationships with Reluctant Learners		■	■				
Brick Math				■	■	■	

Figure 7.2 Sample Training Alignment Map

Training Programs—The Four Levels (2006), Kirkpatrick identifies four distinct levels of evaluation:

- Level 1: Reaction. This level seeks to discover the reactions of training participants to the workshop, program or learning activity being evaluated.
- Level 2: Learning. This level seeks to identify the skills, knowledge and attitudes that participants gained as a result of participating in the training.
- Level 3: Behavioral Change. This advanced level of evaluation seeks to document the extent to which participants applied the training that they received.
- Level 4: Organizational Performance. The most advanced level of evaluation is where the impact on organizational outcomes is documented. In education, a typical organizational outcome would be student achievement and performance. If training focused on strategic talent leadership, outcomes at this level might be decreases in teacher attrition or increases in teacher performance.

School districts have limited budgets. Evaluating 100 percent of training, while a best practice, may not be a viable option. At a minimum, organizations should be collecting data on levels 1 and 2 as this can be completed at no cost during or immediately after the training is delivered. For training that requires a greater investment of time or fiscal resources, evaluation up to levels 3 and 4 are necessary for determining return on investment.

Training Academies Offer Career Pathways

One of my first forays into strategic talent development came when I was offered the opportunity to develop North Carolina's first in-district licensure program for teachers. Using a cohort model, we created an academy for college graduates who were interested in following an alternative pathway into the field of teaching. Annually, a new cohort of beginning teachers spent time together, taking courses in pedagogical practices, participating in professional learning networks, teaching, coaching, attending conferences and engaging in experiential learning activities. The 18-month process afforded them the training and support necessary to achieve their goal of becoming teachers.

Academy and cohort models have many benefits. Because they involve a group of educators, economies of scale can be realized, saving district's time, effort and dollars. But, they also create opportunities for educators to bond together in support of each other as they unite around a common goal. Our results showed that teacher retention for completers of our program was higher than that of traditionally prepared teachers. Interviews with participants revealed with great consistency that it was the cohort model that helped them to persist through challenges. Many school districts are successfully using academy and cohort models to prepare educators for future roles including but not limited to:

- Student Teacher Academy
- Teacher Leader Academy
- Aspiring Leader Academy

Organizations wishing to establish such models can readily find examples of programs across the nation. Some are limited to in-district training, while others represent partnerships with colleges, universities and other school districts. The academy as a form of training is not new and it continues to be a popular format for educators seeking to grow in their practice.

Training is Personalized

In 1984, Malcolm Knowles defined the science of adult learning using the term 'andragogy.' This term is juxtaposed to 'pedagogy,' which, in K-12 education, refers to the science of teaching children. Knowles theory of adult learning began with four assumptions and was later expanded to six underlying assumptions we could make about adults that differentiated them from young learners (Knowles, Holton, & Swanson, 2011):

1. Self-concept
2. (Adult learner) experience
3. Readiness (to learn)
4. Orientation (to learning)
5. Motivation (internal and extrinsic)
6. Need to know

In large group training activities, it would be very challenging to design training that could accommodate all six of these assumptions, ensuring that every adult learner received a fully customizable experience. However, there are ways of expanding training to include additional elements that can address the needs of adult learners. Direct instruction can be accompanied by online modules with learner set goals that are pursued individually and in a job-embedded manner. Adult learners may seek out a coach to provide them with feedback on their application of learning. Learners may even wish to collaborate with other educators to master skills and content. By expanding training designs from single, or sustained, face-to-face training and including additional elements of learning, it is possible for traditional professional development to be personalized for the adult learner (Holcombe, 2000). Strategic Talent Leadership Tool 7—Training Wheels will provide a method for expanding, documenting and evaluating personalized training.

Training is Available to Ancillary Educators

Training is not just for current educators. In fact, the provision of training can serve as a recruiting tool. When I was in a talent development role for a large school district, we used to host nationally known trainers who we knew would draw a large audience. Our strategy was to advertise these big name educators and offer free registration to targeted educators in our region. As a part of the training, we would ensure that recruitment materials were on all tables and that we 'talked-up' the benefits of joining our school district during lunch by planting current employees at each table. The strategy worked beautifully because our current employees participated in the training, our recruits received the benefit of training (which we then benefited from upon hire!) and these prospective hires had the opportunity to ask questions about working in the school district in a low-stress environment over lunch.

Another strategy for realizing exponential value from your training investment includes inviting ancillary educators such as student teachers, substitute teachers and retirees to participate. When student teachers are further engaged in your organization, they become invested in your goals. By including them, at no cost, in all of your development opportunities, you are not only accelerating their effectiveness but sending the message that you value them. This makes the likelihood of them perceiving you as a preferred employer even greater. Similarly, including substitute teachers in training opportunities does not (in most cases) increase your cost, but it does ensure that when these educators are in your classrooms, they have updated training and are more likely to be effective in achieving improved student outcomes. Finally, keeping retirees active in your organization is beneficial for everyone. If a retiree and a beginning teacher are sitting next to each other at a training and form a relationship, you just gained a free mentor for your teacher. If you call upon your retirees to return to the classroom to fill in for leaves of absence or unexpected resignations, they will be up to date on their pedagogical skills. Retirees attending training at no cost might even be willing to volunteer to help coach other teachers as follow-up support after the training as a quid pro quo. And, as another benefit, they are able to keep their licensure up to date. Training should not be viewed as an intervention for current educators only. By expanding the reach of your training, you will ensure the growth of your entire educator community and build good will along the way.

Strategic Talent Leadership Tool 7— Training Wheels

Strategic talent leaders who seek to leverage training opportunities to develop the skills, knowledge and behaviors of educators should challenge themselves to think more broadly than traditional, face-to-face workshops as a singular strategy for training delivery. While there is certainly great value in this format, extensive research has found that training that is sustained over time (50 hours or more) and highly relevant to a teacher's practice can increase student test scores by 21 points (Wei, Darling-Hammond, Adamson, & National Staff Development Council, 2010). In order to achieve relevance, training must move beyond differentiation, varying the 'how,' and individualization, varying the 'when,' to personalization which requires the learner to create their own learning pathway (Basye, 2014).

One way of personalizing learning is to provide educators with a structure they can use to build their own learning pathway. Along this pathway, educators might choose to include multiple training activities such as a face-to-face workshop, coaching, action research and a book study. The multiple activities pathed together toward the achievement of a singular learning outcome will sustain the learning over time. Using the metaphor of a 'training wheel,' Strategic Talent Leadership Tool 7 seeks to support the educator as they are learning how to 'ride' and master their new skill. The circular shape of the training wheel sends the message that the tool is meant to transport them along their learning pathway, bringing forward momentum and progress into the educator's practice. Each training wheel created by an educator requires five simple steps (Figure 7.3):

1. Identify a learning outcome.
2. Identify the training activities that will help to achieve the outcome.

Training Wheel for Questioning Techniques

1. What is your learning outcome for this training wheel?

   I want to be able to use effective questioning techniques with my students.

2. What training strategies will you employ to achieve this outcome?
   a. *I will register for the Effective Questioning and Advanced Questioning workshops (20 hours) offered by our district professional development office.*
   b. *I will engage in a book study about questioning with my teammates as a part of our PLC work.*
   c. *I will spend one week comparing student outcomes between my 1ˢᵗ period, with whom I will use the questioning techniques, and my 4ᵗʰ period with whom I will use my current questioning techniques. I will then analyze the difference in their knowledge retention and performance.*
   d. *I will ask our instructional coach to video me teaching while using the new questioning techniques and will debrief with her after watching the video together.*

3. Using the Training Wheel below, indicate what percentage of your time and effort will be dedicated to each training strategy.

4. How will you evaluate the impact of your learning?

   I will document my new knowledge and skills in a reflective journal. I will apply my new knowledge by participating in book study discussions with my teammates and engaging in a coaching session. Finally, I will compare the differences in student achievement between my two classes to determine the impact of my learning on student achievement outcomes.

5. How many Continuing Education Units you are seeking? *50 hours, 5 CEU's*

   Name and Date: _____

Figure 7.3 Sample Training Wheel

Table 7.3 Action Steps for Training

Best Practice	Data/Resources	Lead	Timeline

3. Using the wheel graphic, allocate the percentage of overall time and effort for each of the selected activities.

4. Describe how impact will be evaluated using Kirkpatrick's four levels.

5. Identify the total time and continuing education units (CEU's) to be documented as a result of completing the training wheel.

Schools and districts using the Training Wheels tool should define practices around how these training activities are initiated, approved, documented and submitted according to district policy.

 ## Action Steps for Training

With your Talent Development Team, identify next steps in becoming more strategic in your training practices.

- Which best practices are you already using to successfully train talent?
- Which new practices would you like to begin implementing?
- In Table 7.3, list new practices for implementation, data/resources needed, a lead team member and the timeline for putting your next steps into action.

 ## Talent Analytics for Training

You have now assessed your current practices and identified some action steps. Following are the talent analytics, found in the Strategic Talent

Leadership Scorecard (Appendix C), that you can use to measure and track your progress toward being a strategic talent leader.

1. Number and percentage of trainings, from all sources, aligned to professional teaching standards and evaluation
2. Number and percentage of trainings evaluated for all four levels of impact
3. Numbers of educators engages in preparation academies for future roles
4. Number of individualized learning experiences completed by role
5. Number of ancillary educators (recruits, substitutes, student teachers, retirees) who participate in training

Case Study Response

Now that you have learned more about best practices for training, what advice would you give to Isabella's principal and district professional development director? Write your response in the space below:

_____

_____

_____

_____

_____

References

Basye, D. (2014). *Personalized vs. differentiated vs. individualized learning*. ISTE. Retrieved from: https://www.iste.org/explore/articleDetail?articleid=124

Holcombe, A. (2000). *Technology Staff Development- Facilitators and Barriers to Online Learning* (Doctoral Dissertation, University of North Carolina at Greensboro, Greensboro, USA).

Kirkpatrick, D., & Kirkpatrick, J. (2006). *Evaluating training programs: The four levels*. Oakland, CA: Berrett-Koehler Publishers.

Knowles, M., Holton, E., & Swanson, R. (2011). *The adult learner: The definitive classic in adult education and human resource development* (7th ed.). Amsterdam; Boston: Elsevier, Butterworth-Heinemann.

The New Teacher Project. (2015). *The mirage: Confronting the hard truth about our quest for teacher development*. Brooklyn, NY: TNTP. Retrieved from http://tntp.org/assets/documents/TNTP-Mirage_2015.pdf

Wei, R., Darling-Hammond, L. Adamson, F., & National Staff Development Council. (2010). *Professional development in the United States: Trends and challenges. Phase II of a three-phase study*. National Staff Development Center.

8 | Coaching

Maggie Chavis was frustrated. She knew that when she accepted a job teaching language arts at a highly impacted middle school, designated as 'low performing' by the state, that her job would not be easy. But, she was an experienced and accomplished teacher with a solid record of helping students gain 1.5+ years of growth per year. Maggie loved her students and truly enjoyed teaching every day. The grading was a lot, but that was to be expected for a language arts teacher. What was overwhelming Maggie was not the typical workload of a teacher, it was the endless stream of coaches coming in and out of her classroom, telling her what to do. On Monday, her principal and curriculum facilitator did walkthroughs, leaving behind notes about what to improve. On Tuesdays and Thursdays, the literacy coaches from central office observed all language arts teachers and held coaching sessions with them after school. The English as a Second or Other Language (ESOL) coach stopped by intermittently to make sure that Maggie was addressing the needs of her seven ESOL students. And, the state-assigned, low-performing schools, coach dropped in several times a week and insisted upon meeting with Maggie during her planning period. One day last week, three coaches showed up in her room during the same class period! Was this really the type of support she needed? It seemed to her like there were too many people giving advice but not enough doing the work!

Coaching Talent

Coaching is the practice of providing nonevaluative feedback designed to improve performance. Much like athletic coaching, professional coaching can be delivered peer to peer or expert to novice. The critical distinction between coaching and evaluation is that coaching is nonpunitive. It is best done using a consistent framework or approach across an organization. Individualized coaching has one of the highest returns on investment within education and is backed up by substantial data showing positive impacts on student achievement outcomes. Coaching is a critical part of any strategic talent leadership approach.

Impacts of Coaching

In 1978, Vygotsky defined the Zone of Proximal Development (ZPD) as "the distance between the actual developmental level as determined by independent problem solving and the level of potential development as determined through problem solving under adult guidance, or in collaboration with more capable peers" (p. 86). It is through that adult guidance, or coaching, that strategic talent leaders seek to help educators become more effective. It is estimated that across the United States, school districts spend $8 billion, annually, on training and support (The New Teacher Project, 2015). And, coaching represents a significant portion of this budget, as the typical investment in coaching includes the salaries and benefits of those providing the support. A recent meta-analysis of 60 research studies that investigated the impact of coaching on instruction and student outcomes yielded very promising results. Across these studies, all of which employed a causal research design, investigators calculated a pooled effect size of 0.49 standard deviations on instruction and a smaller, 0.18 standard deviation on student achievement outcomes (Kraft, Blazer, & Hogan, 2018). This is the most recent evidence we have that coaching causes educators to improve in their practice.

While types of coaching support may vary school to school and district to district, the purpose remains the same—to close the gap between the acquisition of new skills and knowledge and the application of them (Showers, 1985). Some common coaching roles include school improvement, instructional, beginning teacher, content, data, behavior management, special education, ESOL, executive and leadership. Regardless of the type of coaching provided, there are some common traits of coaches whose work yields positive impacts on coachees and their students (Joyce & Showers, 2003; Knight, 2017; Pierce, 2015;Vermont Agency of Education; 2016). Effective coaches:

- believe that the educator can improve in their practice;
- value relationships and trust;

- maintain confidentiality;
- exhibit effective communication skills;
- summarize and ask open-ended questions;
- have the ability to break down practice into its component parts;
- provide goal specific, targeted, feedback and
- listen more than talk.

When coaches employ these traits for the good of educator improvement, coaching may serve as "the most effective intervention designed for human performance" (Gawande, 2011).

Strategic Talent Leadership Insights for Coaching

With your Strategic Talent Leadership Team, review the strategic talent leadership practices for coaching (see Table 8.1). If you are currently engaging in a practice, check 'yes.' If not, check 'not yet' and consider how this practice could be adopted by your organization as you read through the best practices described in this chapter.

Table 8.1 Strategic Talent Leadership Insights for Coaching

Strategic Practice	Yes	Not Yet
Our organization assesses coaching needs.		
Our organization identifies and trains coaches in a variety of areas such as executive coaching for leaders, instructional coaching for teachers and targeted coaching for job performance.		
Our organization facilitates fulfilling educator requests for appropriately trained coaches.		
Our organization ensures that all coaches set, track and measure goal achievement in collaboration with educators.		
Our organization provides coaches with release time or monetary compensation.		

Best Practices for Coaching Talent

Assess Your Coaching Needs

In our case study example, it is clear that no one has assessed Maggie's need for coaching. While a struggling, beginning teacher may need intensive mentoring, a form of coaching, an experienced and accomplished teacher may need a career coach who can help her to develop her leadership skillset. Allocating coaching resources without a strategy is not only inefficient, it can cause harm by underserving those in the greatest need and overserving those who are already effective. The resulting collateral damage of providing coaching without a plan can be decreased in job satisfaction, toxic working conditions and even teacher attrition.

Strategic talent leaders wishing to create effective coaching programs must first know who needs to be coached and in which areas. Once that information is available, coaching ratios can be set based upon the organization's budget and coaches can be assigned. Table 8.2 illustrates how coaching needs can quickly be assessed by calculating the total number of educators who need coaching, by area of need and allocating coaches at a ratio of 1:25 for one hour of service per week.

Once you understand the number of full-time equivalent coaches needed to provide a baseline of one hour per week of support, you can begin to assess whether or not you have access to the right coaches. Master

Table 8.2 Sample Coaching Needs Assessment

Coaching Needs	Number of Teachers in Need of Coaching	Number of Coaches Needed (1:25, 1 hr/week)
Beginning teacher	148	6
ESOL support	53	2
SPED support	88	3.5
Classroom management	103	4
Instructional effectiveness	80	3
Content—Math	19	1
Content—Literacy	27	1
New leader	10	0.5
Total Coaching Full-time Equivalents (FTE's) Needed:		**21.5**

teachers with a background in SPED should be able to serve teachers in special education as well as provide service to teachers who need help with classroom management or instructional effectiveness. Coaches do not have to be designated as purely one 'type' of coach so long as they have an understanding of all types of support services they have been assigned to provide to specific teachers. By hiring coaches who can support multiple coaching needs, you gain greater flexibility and even the option of finding a 1:25 ratio within a single school, allowing you to assign a coach to only one school. Regardless of how you allocate your coaching resources, the key is to do so with a strategy in mind that ensures that everyone who needs to be supported is, and that resources are not wasted on those who are not in need of coaching or do not want to be coached.

Cultivate Coaching Expertise

As described in Table 8.2, educators require coaching in a variety of areas. Do you currently have coaches trained to provide support in each of them? Many districts not only lack the coaching expertise breadth that they need but also lack an agreed-upon approach to coaching. In all of the site-based assessments I've completed in school districts across the country, not a single one has used an agreed-upon method for providing coaching to educators. In total, I've observed districts using coaching to address the following needs:

- Assessment (formative and summative)
- Beginning teachers
- Classroom management
- Content (math, literacy, science)
- Data
- ESOL
- Executive coaching
- Instructional effectiveness
- Leadership (teacher leaders and new principals)
- SPED
- Technology

With the range of coaching occurring nationally, it is not surprising that districts have not chosen a single approach. And yet, identifying a framework for coaching would help those on the receiving end make greater sense of the recommendations being made. In real life, Maggie (not her real name, of course) was told on the same day to USE and NOT USE the very same strategy with her students. Were her coaches working from the same coaching framework, this would not have been an issue. A sampling of popular coaching models and frameworks currently in broad use across the nation includes:

- Diane Sweeney's Student-Centered Coaching
- Elena Aguilar's approach as described in *The Art of Coaching*
- Jim Knight's model for Instructional Coaching
- Michael Bungay Stanier's, *The Coaching Habit*
- The New Teacher Center's model for teacher induction, instructional coaching and school leadership
- TNTP's beginning teacher training

As strategic talent leaders, successful coaching must first include defining the coaching needs that you are able to provide. Next, select a coaching framework for each type of support you intend to provide and ensure that all of the coaches you deploy are fully trained prior to being deployed into schools and classroom. Anything less will fall short of the potential coaching yields for increasing educator effectiveness.

Ensure Maximum Coaching Access

If access to monetary resources were not a factor, strategic talent leaders would provide every teacher, leader and employee a coach for the purpose of helping them to reflect upon and improve their practice. Unfortunately, in education (and in most industries), we are not well enough resourced. But, we should not let the absence of unlimited resources deter us from maximizing access to coaches for all educators. "No matter how well trained people are; few can sustain their best performance on their own." (Gawande, 2011). In planning a maximum access coaching program for your organization, some questions to consider include:

- Do you have educators who want to be coached? Are they willing to receive feedback?

- Do you currently have coaches who are trained and have experience working with adult learners?

- Knowing that coaching resources are limited, how will you prioritize who gets coached?

- Are you willing to ensure that your coaches can preserve confidentiality?

- Are you willing to dedicate time for coaches to meet regularly with coachees?

- Will coaches use specific, measurable target goals and metrics to track progress?

Once you have considered these program design questions, you are ready to make your program available to your school and district. When launching your coaching program, it will be important to destigmatize coaching as, historically, this type of support may have been designated for struggling educators only. Ensure that in your messaging, you clearly communicate that coaching is for anyone seeking to grow in their practice, whether a beginning teacher, experienced professional or current leader. Finally, design procedures for making a coaching request and fulfilling the match between coach and coachee. Table 8.3 describes some of

Table 8.3 Coaching Roles and Responsibilities

Coach's Responsibility	Educator's Responsibility
Listen	Initiate coaching request
Keep coaching appointments	Keep coaching appointments
Maintain confidentiality	Exhibit coachability
Ask good questions	Share openly
Provide viable options when asked	Own your growth
Model when appropriate	Observe model practices
Co-teach when appropriate	Co-teach when appropriate
Track progress	Track impact

the responsibilities your coachees may want to consider when making a request for a coach to be assigned.

Measure the Impact of Coaching

Once coaches and coachees are matched and working together, it will be important to collect data about the impact of their efforts. To measure impact, coaching efforts have to be targeted to specific outcomes. While a beginning teacher might say, '*I need help with everything,*' it is the role of the coach to discern prioritized needs and name them. That does not mean that coachee choice it eliminated, it merely means that the coach is able to respond to general requests by offering options for where to begin. They may use language such as, '*I understand that you are open to being coached on a variety of needs. In my experience, it helps to focus on one at a time. Is there something that you feel is more important to you right now?*' If the coachee is unable to identify a first step, the coach can then make a few suggestions and prompt the teacher to select one.

After the identification of a targeted goal, the coach and coachee will proceed to identify and practice a strategy followed by the evaluation of results. Upon reflection, and revisions to practice, if necessary, the cycle begins again as illustrated in Figure 8.1.

Educators who activate a request for coaching may only want to go through one coaching cycle to target a specific need. Or, they may want to create an entire pathway of skills that lead to improved performance. Whether short- or long-term access to a coach is requested, Strategic Talent Leadership Tool 8—Capture the Learning, will aid in documenting the impacts of efforts.

Compensate Coaches

Many districts are able to provide support to their educators through the use of full-time coaches who do not have teaching or administrative duties. Others leverage consultants who are external to the district but are contracted to provide prescribed coaching support to targeted groups of educators. And, still others rely upon employees with full-time duties to coach others during their planning time, before school, after

Figure 8.1 Coaching Cycle

school or virtually. No matter the arrangement, it is important that those team members who provide valuable coaching and support receive compensation.

This compensation can come in many forms. For those educators who are full-time coaches, benefits and salary serve as compensation. But, for the population of coaches that are performing coaching duties in addition to their regular job role, some compensation considerations are:

- extended employment contracts or additional pay for the additional work;
- reduced course load, allowing for an additional planning period that can be used to provide coaching; or
- trade days which allow coaches to take vacation on teacher workdays in exchange for time already worked in the form of coaching before/ after school or during their planning period.

Another model gaining popularity due to its positive impacts on student achievement is the use of multi-classroom leaders. The Opportunity

Culture model, created by Dr. Bryan Hassel, co-director at Public Impact, leverages existing school and district funding to create teacher leader positions that provide additional support to teachers, including the provision of coaching. Teachers supported by a multi-classroom leader were able to move students from the 50th percentile up to the 72nd percentile in reading and 85th in math. While this study was of a single large district in the southeast, early results from districts across the country are showing similar impacts. Strategic talent leaders leverage the value of coaching and training, ideally in combination, to maximize opportunities for educators to grow and increase in their effectiveness.

Strategic Talent Leadership Tool 8—Capture the Learning

Considering the resources districts dedicate to providing educators with one-on-one coaching and support, the need to demonstrate a return on investment is great. Because the coaching relationship is between two individuals, capturing the learning and documenting impact is more entailed than reporting a single metric at the end of the school year. That is why Strategic Talent Leadership Tool 8—Capture the Learning was created (Figure 8.2). When I first used this tool in a large urban district, we created a web-based portal to collect the information, making it easier to run reports that showed impact data by coach, by school, by coaching strategy and even professional teaching standard. But, it works just as well as a low-tech tool, documented on paper and analyzed teacher-by-teacher at the end of the school year.

In the Sample Capture the Learning, you can see that this is Maggie's second attempt at achieving her target goal. While she made progress, she and her coach have decided to launch a third coaching cycle in order to reach mastery. Some goals may only take a single cycle to master, while others may take multiple cycles. By using the Capture the Learning tool, coachees and their coaches can track progress along their pathway to mastery. At the end of the school year, coaching cycles can be easily summarized by analyzing the total amount of support,

Capture the Learning		
Teacher	*Maggie Rangel*	
Coach	*Nic Houser*	
Date and Time of Session:	*February 22, 2:30-3:30*	
Targeted Goal	*Reduce the transition time between activities to <30 seconds in order to gain additional teaching and learning time.*	
Alignment to Standards	**Professional Teaching Standards**		
	☐ 1a	☐ 2a	☐ 3a
	☑ 1b	☐ 2b	☐ 3b
	☐ 1c	☑ 2c	☐ 3c
		☑ 2d	
Coaching Cycle	2	
Strategy Selected	*Use of a hand signal, verbal transition cue, and clear directions*	
Strategy Practice	☐ Observed in a master teacher's classroom ☐ Modeled by coach ☐ Co-taught with coach ☑ Video-taped practice and viewed with coach ☑ Use of a checklist ☐ Other: _____	
Results	☐ Goal Met ☑ Goal Not Yet Met *Maggie was able to reduce her transition time from 2 minutes, as documented in the first coaching cycle, down to under 1 minute this time. Her goal is to spend no more than 30 seconds on each transition.*	
Next Steps	*Initiate a 3rd coaching cycle. This next cycle will involve observing a master teacher and replicating her use of signals.*	

Figure 8.2 Sample Capture the Learning

number of coaching cycles, standards addressed, goals met and by any other data point deemed valuable to the school or district. For easy analysis, this document can be made into an electronic form that feeds into a database. Or, for analyzing thousands of coaching cycles, you can always explore the use of a web-based portal with robust reporting tools.

Table 8.4 Action Steps for Coaching

Best Practice	Data/Resources	Lead	Timeline

Action Steps for Coaching

With your Talent Development Team, identify next steps in becoming more strategic in your coaching practices.

- Which best practices are you already using to successfully coach talent?
- Which new practices would you like to begin implementing?
- In Table 8.4, list new practices for implementation, data/resources needed, a lead team member and the timeline for putting your next steps into action.

Talent Analytics for Coaching

You have now assessed your current practices and identified some action steps. Below are the talent analytics, found in the Strategic Talent Leadership Scorecard (Appendix C), that you can use to measure and track your progress toward being a strategic talent leader.

1. Number of educators who need coaching by target area
2. Number of coaches trained and available by target area
3. Number and percentage of coaching requests fulfilled
4. Number of coaching goals achieved
5. Number of coaches compensated by method

Case Study Response

Now that you have learned more about best practices for coaching educators, what advice would you give to Maggie's principal and district coaching coordinator? Write your response in the space below:

_____

_____

_____

_____

_____

References

Gawande, A. (2011). Personal best. Top athletes and singers have coaches. Should you? *Annals of Medicine*, October, 2011.

Joyce, B., & Showers, B. (2002). *Student achievement through staff development (3rd Edition)*. Alexandria, VA: Association for Supervision and Curriculum Development.

Knight, J. (2017). *The impact cycle: What instructional coaches should do to foster powerful improvements in teaching*. Thousand Oaks, CA: Corwin.

Kraft, M., Blazer, D., & Hogan, D. (2018). The effect of teacher coaching on instruction and achievement: A meta-analysis of the causal evidence. *Review of Educational Research*, *88*(4), pp. 547–588. Retrieved from: https://journals.sagepub.com.libproxy.highpoint.edu/doi/pdf/10.3102/0034654318759268

Pierce, J. D. (2015). *Teacher-coach alliance as a critical component of coaching: Effects of feedback and analysis on teacher practice* (Doctoral dissertation, University of Washington). Retrieved from http://hdl.handle.net/1773/33786

Showers, B. (1985). Teachers coaching teachers. *Education Leadership*, April, 1985: ASCD.

The New Teacher Project. (2015). *The mirage: Confronting the hard truth about our quest for teacher development.* Brooklyn, NY: TNTP. Retrieved from: http://tntp.org/assets/documents/TNTP-Mirage_2015.pdf

Vermont Agency of Education. (2016). *Coaching as professional learning: Guidance for implementing effective coaching systems.* Vermont Agency of Education. Retrieved from: https://eric.ed.gov/?id=ED573000

Vygotsky, L. (1978). *Mind in society: The development of higher psychological processes.* Cambridge, MA: Harvard University Press.

Evaluating

9

It had been a tough first year for Aanya Kumar, but she was looking forward to the summer break and spending a few weeks visiting her family at the coast where she grew up. She liked her school and had largely depended upon her teammates for support as she struggled with discipline, the overwhelming challenge of keeping up with lesson planning, and learning about how to best use formative assessment data. Aanya's principal, Ulises Rivera was nice enough. He popped his head in Aanya's door once in a while to say hello to the class and watch her in action. She didn't know what to expect when she arrived in Mr. Rivera's office for her summative evaluation but knew that she had made drastic improvements since her first day of school. With a nervous smile, she sat down across the table from Mr. Rivera and picked up a copy of her evaluation. On standard after standard, she was rated as not satisfactory! How could this person who had never seen her teach for more than five minutes at a time be a good judge of her performance? She did her best to pay attention while he was explaining the areas she was to improve for next year, but all Aanya could think about was whether or not she should come back after her family vacation.

Evaluating Talent

Evaluating is the practice of providing feedback to employees in relation to a set of professional standards and expectations. Summative evaluations can comprise multiple data sets including but not limited to classroom observations, student performance at the classroom, team and school levels, professionalism, content knowledge, pedagogical practice and student surveys. Most summative evaluations highlight current employee strengths but also offer areas for continued improvement and development. A strong evaluation process should differentiate highly effective employees from average and underperforming employees. Unlike developmental feedback, evaluative feedback requires that an employee respond to recommendations by changing their behavior.

A well-managed evaluation program is a critical part of leading a strong talent strategy. While evaluation's most traditional purpose is to provide formal feedback to educators using a standardized set of performance expectations with the end goal of improving performance, a secondary function is to use evaluation output data to inform future training, coaching, promotion, compensation and retention decisions. Principals and hiring managers may even use evaluation data in consideration of hiring a new employee. Evaluations serve as a proxy to being in a classroom, watching a teacher perform his/her craft. As such, the goal is for them to accurately reflect practice and differentiate effectiveness among teachers.

The Evolution of Teacher Evaluation

Educators have been engaged in performance evaluation for centuries. Evaluations from the 19th and 20th centuries often included comments about morality, church attendance, appearance (several evaluations I reviewed included comments about a teacher's lipstick being 'too red') as well as the provision of community service in addition to teaching duties. Over the years, evaluations let go of lipstick color as a determinant of teacher quality and began to align to local, state and national models of professional teaching standards. Even so, they continued to follow a fairly typical model of annual evaluations for beginning teachers and for experienced teachers, an evaluation once every three or four years.

That all changed with the launch of No Child Left Behind (NCLB) 2002 followed by release of Race to the Top grant funds in 2009. Both national efforts sought to reform education by placing a greater emphasis on principal and teacher effectiveness through rigorous, transparent and fair evaluation systems. As a result, states across the nation reformed their evaluation systems to include components of student performance (Mead, Rotherham, Brown, & American Enterprise Institute for Public

Policy Research, 2012). States that applied for waivers for some of the NCLB provisions had to agree to:

- evaluate educators on a regular basis;

- support instructional improvement;

- differentiate performance using at least three levels;

- incorporate multiple measures of educator performance, including student growth as a significant factor;

- provide clear, timely and useful feedback to inform professional development; and

- use evaluations to inform personnel decisions (US Department of Education, 2011)

The laws and penalties tied to federal educations dollars spurned the greatest shift in educational practice and policy since the signing of the Elementary and Secondary Education Act in 1965. These reforms brought national attention to the practices of human capital management in education. The Strategic Talent Leadership Framework is heavily based upon these reforms, calling for the alignment of all human resources functions in support of improved outcomes for our students.

In the same year as the release of the $4.35 billion in Race to the Top grants, TNTP published *The Widget Effect*, a report that dovetailed perfectly with national education priorities. Highlighted in this study was the failure of current evaluation systems to identify ineffective teachers. Less than 1 percent of the 40,000 evaluations reviewed in the study revealed unsatisfactory teacher performance (Weisberg, Sexton, Mulhern, & Keeling, 2009). From a talent leadership perspective, this is detrimental in multiple ways—for underperforming teachers, it reinforces ineffective behaviors, fails to identify areas for training and coaching support and continues to expose fragile students to instruction that, over time, will only ensure that they are not prepared for a career or college. "In fact, 73 percent of teachers surveyed said their most recent evaluation did not identify any development areas, and only 45 percent of teachers who did have development areas identified said they received useful support to improve" (Weisberg et al., 2009, p. 6). The result—the inability of our evaluation systems to differentiate among the effectiveness levels of the very resource, talent, which has the greatest impact upon student achievement outcomes. To counteract these impacts, Weisberg and his team identified four best practices:

– Adopt a comprehensive performance evaluation system that fairly, accurately and credibly differentiates teachers based on their effectiveness in promoting student achievement.
– Train administrators and other evaluators in the teacher performance evaluation system and hold them accountable for using it effectively.
– Integrate the performance evaluation system with critical human capital policies and functions such as teacher assignment, professional development, compensation, retention and dismissal.
– Adopt dismissal policies that provide lower-stakes options for ineffective teachers to exit the district and a system of due process that is fair but efficient.

These recommendations, in conjunction with the release of Race to the Top federal dollars, sent a clear message to states and local education agencies across the nation that lipstick would forevermore be absent as a determinant of teacher effectiveness! In support of *The Widget Effect* and its dire findings, TNTP released, one year later, *Teacher Evaluation 2.0*, a set of recommendations for improving the teacher evaluation and feedback mechanisms currently being implemented (The New Teacher Project, 2010). Their recommendations included annual evaluations for all teachers, evaluations that address pre-identified expectations that 'prioritize student learning,' the use of multiple measures, a rations scale inclusive of four to five levels and the provision of regular feedback to all teachers. Their final recommendation was the most controversial in that it suggested that evaluation ratings should be considered in decisions to employ and retain teachers.

Immediately following the publication of these two seminal reports by TNTP, the Bill and Melinda Gates Foundation launched the *Measuring Effective Teaching Project* (MET). The goal of this study was to analyze data from thousands of classrooms in order to determine whether or not characteristics of effective teaching and/or teachers could be isolated. An analysis of 3,000+ classrooms concluded that

85 percent of the teachers were 'remarkably similar' in their practices (Cantrell, 2012). Although, the researchers were hoping to identify replicable practices that could lead to improved practice nationally, they did resolve that there were some practices around evaluation behaviors that could make the investment of time more valuable (Bill and Melinda Gates Foundation, 2013):

- Use student perception surveys.
- Create trust in the evaluation process by defining and adhering to specific procedures.
- Ensure that evaluators are well-trained and that they calibrate their practices.
- Use multiple data sources to inform final evaluation ratings.
- Take a balanced approach to weighting those data sources.
- Leverage video as a method of providing teachers with feedback and for training evaluators (also a strong recommendation of Jim Knight).

Educator evaluation has transformed in practice from single evaluator ratings to the inclusion of multiple measures. Less transformation has occurred, however, in the application of evaluation outcomes for informing other strategic talent practices such as training, coaching, compensation, promotion and retention. The purpose of this chapter is not to help you re-create your current evaluation system, rather, to nudge you into thinking about how you use your evaluation results as a part of the broader strategic talent leadership framework.

Strategic Talent Leadership Insights for Evaluating

With your Strategic Talent Leadership Team, review the strategic talent leadership practices for evaluating (see Table 9.1). If you are currently engaging in a practice, check 'yes.' If not, check 'not yet' and consider how this practice could be adopted by your organization as you read through the best practices described in this chapter.

Table 9.1 Strategic Talent Leadership Insights for Evaluating

Strategic Practice	Yes	Not Yet
Our organization provides regular training to evaluators to ensure consistency in practices.		
Our organization conducts cross-tab analyses to identify instances of overestimated and underestimated teacher performance.		
Our organization uses teacher evaluation ratings to make strategic student assignments to benefit the most fragile students.		
Our organization tracks and analyzes evaluation results by licensure granting college/university.		
Our organization uses evaluation results to inform other talent functions such as hiring, training, coaching, promotion and retention.		

Best Practices for Evaluating Talent

Train Evaluators and Calibrate Practice

I still recall teacher workroom conversations during which my peers would lament their evaluator assignment for the year. It was well known that Assistant Principal A was an 'easier' evaluator than Assistant Principal B, making him the preferred evaluator. The real conversation should have been around which administrator provided the best feedback and support. Inevitably, there will be some variance in evaluator ratings as not every lesson is delivered with the exact level of expertise as every other lesson. We all have our 'on' and 'off' days of teaching and individual observation data should reflect such. But, there should be a level of predictable consistency across our practice and strong evaluation systems and evaluators should be able to capture that practice.

To accurately capture the practice of teaching and learning in an evaluation takes training. Strategic talent leaders ensure that all evaluators have received sufficient training prior to being deployed into classrooms, observing and providing feedback to teachers. Whether observing through nonevaluative walkthroughs or conducting formal evaluation observations, the person tasked with judging the effectiveness of an educator must be well versed in the system designed to capture behaviors and the craft of debriefing his/her ratings with the educator. This includes having a deep understanding of the conceptual framework underlying the evaluation system as well as possessing the ability to provide specific and measurable feedback to the observed educator. A study from the American Enterprise Institute for Public Policy Research (2011) recommends that evaluator training includes examples of teaching, preferably videos, as a part of the training and calibration. Before being deployed into classrooms, they recommend that evaluators pass a certification test to ensure accuracy in ratings. Finally, the use of year-long calibration of ratings should be used to ensure inter-rater reliability. Only then can we be assured that the evaluation data is a reliable and valid source of information for driving other human capital decisions.

Strive for Evaluation Rating and Student Performance Congruence

When evaluation practices meaningfully differentiate between effective and ineffective educators, evaluation ratings and student performance outcomes should be congruent. The use of a cross-tab analysis allows for the analysis of the relationship between variables. In this case, we would like to compare teacher evaluation ratings and student performance rating. The source of this data will vary by school district that may need to be translated into a numerical value. In the example below (Table 9.2), Student Value-Added Data Level is the student performance variable (1 = Does not meet growth projections, 5 = Exceeds growth projections) and Teacher

Table 9.2 Sample Cross-Tab Analysis for Teacher Evaluation and Student Performance

Student VAD Level	Teacher Evaluation Rating				
	1	2	3	4	5
5	0	1	5	4	3
4	1	0	4	2	4
3	0	1	7	3	1
2	1	3	6	2	0
1	2	5	4	1	2

Evaluation Rating is the teacher performance variable (1 = Unsatisfactory, 5 = Exceptional).

If teacher evaluation ratings and student Value Added Data (VAD) levels were in perfect alignment, top-performing teachers would be rated a '5' and their students would be earning the highest VAD growth level of '5.' In this example, there are three teachers who are rated a '5' whose students are achieving at a VAD Level 5. Likewise, the lowest performing teachers would be rated a '1' and their students would not be achieving expected growth as indicated by a VAD level of '1.' In this example, there are two teachers who are rated a '1' whose students are achieving at a VAD Level 1. But, this analysis also reveals instances of both over- and underestimated performance (as indicated by the shaded cells). There are teachers whose ratings are at Levels 1 and 2 whose students are achieving above expected levels of growth at VAD Levels 4 and 5, representing an underestimation of teacher effectiveness. And, there are teachers whose ratings are at Levels 4 and 5 whose students are not meeting expected growth as indicated by their VAD Levels 1 and 2, representing an overestimation of teacher effectiveness. While both misalignments are undesirable, it is far worse to overestimate a teacher's effectiveness, giving them a false sense of efficacy and ensuring that they will only continue their current practice. Table 9.3 more easily illustrates both scenarios.

Well-trained evaluators will always land in quadrants one (High/High) and three (Low/Low). It is when there is congruence between teacher and student performance that valid conversations about teacher effectiveness can occur. Over- and underestimating teacher performance makes evaluation feedback extremely confusing to the teacher and will, in the case of overestimated performance, lead to continued ineffective teacher

Table 9.3 Over- and Underestimated Teacher Effectiveness

		Teacher Evaluation Ratings	
		−	+
Student Value Added Data Levels	+	**Underestimated Performance** High VAD Low Evaluation	High VAD High Evaluation
	−	Low VAD Low Evaluation	**Overestimated Performance** Low VAD High Evaluation

performance and, in the case of underestimated performance, lead to job dissatisfaction and possibly teacher migration.

Consider Evaluation Data in Making Student Assignments

Teacher evaluations should be a primary considering when scheduling students. And, in order to consider this data, student scheduling cannot be left to a software program that randomizes student assignments. It must be done by hand and in conjunction with historical student assignment patterns. Take, for example, the student assignment patterns in Table 9.4. Benedicto was assigned to a low-performing teacher in the 3rd, 4th and 6th grades and to an average-performing teacher in the 5th grade. His cohort peers were randomly assigned to different student assignment patterns.

Which student do you think has the strongest chance of performing well in the 7th grade, graduating on time and getting into college? In an extensive study of student assignment patterns, June Rivers and William Sanders (1996) discovered that after a three-year teacher assignment sequence, student achievement differences could vary by over 50 percentile points. In comparing two different school districts, the patterns that emerged were similar (Table 9.5).

Even if Romi and Michael started out at the same achievement level, with the same 3rd-grade teacher, their assignments the proceeding three years could change their life trajectories. "If we only took the simple step of assuring that poor and minority children had highly qualified teachers, about half of the achievement gap would disappear" (Haycock, 1998). One of the reasons that this is not often done is that it is time consuming. Principals need to create historical teacher assignment sequences (or use a tool such as the Educator Value-Added Assessment System that provides this reporting) to ensure that no student, especially not our most fragile

Table 9.4 Sample Student Assignment Patterns

Student	3rd Grade	4th Grade	5th Grade	6th Grade
Benedicto	LOW	LOW	AVERAGE	LOW
Romi	AVERAGE	HIGH	HIGH	HIGH
Michael	AVERAGE	LOW	LOW	LOW

Table 9.5 Comparison of Student Assignment Sequences

District	LOW-LOW-LOW	HIGH-HIGH-HIGH	Difference
A	44th percentile	96th percentile	52 percentile points
B	29th percentile	83rd percentile	54 percentile points

students, is assigned to a low-performing teacher two years in a row. In fact, Haycock and others agree that if our most fragile students were assigned to sequences of only high-performing teachers, we could eliminate the achievement gap altogether.

Track Educator Performance by Degree and Licensure Granting College/University

Every town has a place that everyone knows has the best pizza, Mexican food, seafood, etc. But, do you know who has the best teacher candidates? You should. As shared earlier in the book, there are only two ways to create a faculty of highly effective teachers—hire effective teachers onto your faculty or develop the effectiveness of the teachers you have. Some may argue that it's difficult to judge the effectiveness of beginning teachers as they have not yet generated measurable outcomes. On the contrary, an examination of the historical effectiveness of teacher candidates graduated and/or licensed by colleges and universities can offer rich insight into the potential effectiveness of a candidate. I worked on a team in a large district that attempted to do this. We exported five years of hiring data from our HR core system into Excel. We then exported the Value-Added Data (VAD) for those teachers into that same spreadsheet. After a little data scrubbing, we were able to analyze the average VAD score for candidates by degree and licensure granting organization. In the sample data set, you can see that some universities are generating students that perform above expected growth (VAD score of 3) and others fall short (Table 9.6).

When our local colleges and universities heard that we were tracking this data, they became highly interested in how their students compared to their competitors. Our team was even more interested because our goal was to hire as many teachers as we could from those organizations that were preparing the most effective teachers. Armed with this data, we were

Table 9.6 Sample Teacher VAD by Degree or Licensure Granting University

College or University	Average VAD after 1 year	Average VAD after 2 years	Average VAD after 3 years	Average VAD after 4 years
A	2.9	3.2	3.1	3.1
B	3.1	3.3	3.8	3.8
C	2.7	2.7	2.8	3.0
D	3.5	3.6	4.1	4.2
E	3.8	3.6	4.0	4.1

better able to leverage our recruiting dollars to target universities D and E, helping our principals to build teams of effective teachers.

Leverage Evaluation Data to Inform Practices in Other HR Functions

The entire purpose of the evaluating process is to generate information. This sets evaluating apart from all other functions other than forecasting. In response to an analysis of evaluation data, we can:

- provide feedback to teachers as a means of making them more aware of their practice;
- prescribe the providing of training;
- assign a coach to help the educator improve their practice;
- make a promotion based upon continued exceptional performance;
- make a recommendation to award tenure or an extension of employment contract;
- recommend a different job assignment for the educator; or
- compensate the educator at a higher rate in an effort to retain their talents.

There are so many uses for evaluation data at the individual, school and district levels. In Chapter 7, Training, we saw a sample alignment of training courses to professional teaching standards. At a district level, an analysis of evaluation results across the district and by school can inform the allocation of training dollars for the following school year. For example, if

65 percent of teachers in School A were rated 'unsatisfactory' in classroom management, we can work with that principal to bring additional training and coaching support to those teachers. And, if School B's evaluation ratings on the use of formative assessment are outstanding, we know that we can cancel the consultant we have scheduled to come and provide training or maybe redirect her to School C who happens to be struggling with formative assessment. Not unlike how we use student performance data to personalize teaching and learning for our young people, evaluation data can provide us with the tools we need to personalize development for our adults.

Strategic Talent Leadership Tool 9—9-Box Talent Review

The Strategic Talent Leadership Tool—9-Box Talent Review—is one resource that can support our efforts to better understand the needs of our educators. When we have an increased understanding of what teachers like Aanya, our case study subject, need, we can use that data to be more responsive and supportive of their growth. The 9-Box Talent Review helps principals and district leaders to look at employees in relation to each other. By classifying the current and potential performance of each team member, we gain an understanding of the overall strength of our organization and of similar-performing individuals. This allows us to make better strategic talent decisions with our time, effort, staffing and funding resources. Instead of continuously dumping all of our resources into our most struggling educators, the 9-Box Talent Review tool forces us to pay attention to the needs of all team members. If we do not embrace a strategy that nudges our highest performers into leadership roles and average performers into improved practice, we will have expended all of our resources on those employees who yield us the least benefit.

To populate the 9-Box Talent Review tool (Figure 9.1), administrators should first consider current employee performance and distribute names across the nine boxes. In a second review, consider the future potential performance of the team member. Will they remain in place? Can they move up one level of scope and responsibility? Or, do they have the potential to keep moving up, ever increasing their level of influence? One placed, team member assignments to boxes can then be used to determine what

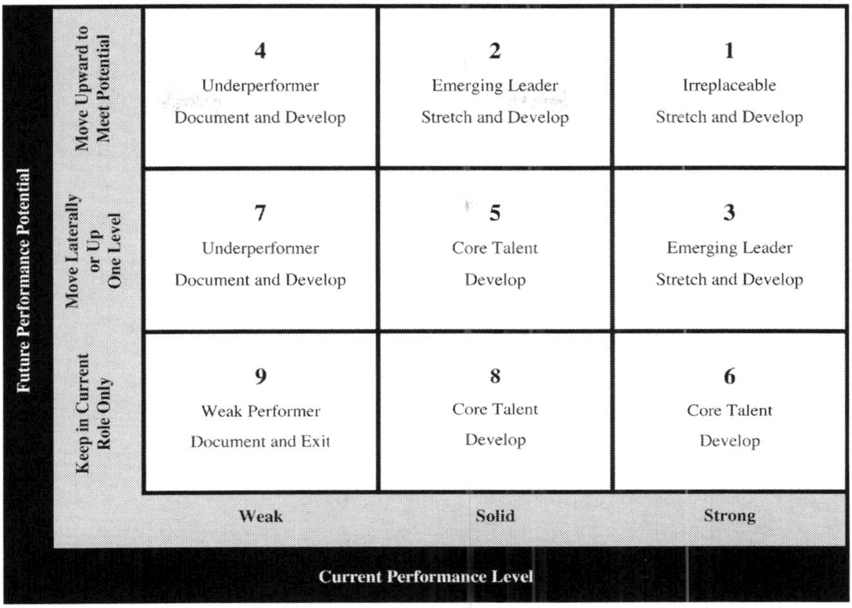

	Weak	Solid	Strong
Move Upward to Meet Potential	**4** Underperformer — Document and Develop	**2** Emerging Leader — Stretch and Develop	**1** Irreplaceable — Stretch and Develop
Move Laterally or Up One Level	**7** Underperformer — Document and Develop	**5** Core Talent — Develop	**3** Emerging Leader — Stretch and Develop
Keep in Current Role Only	**9** Weak Performer — Document and Exit	**8** Core Talent — Develop	**6** Core Talent — Develop

(Future Performance Potential — vertical axis; Current Performance Level — horizontal axis)

Figure 9.1 9-Box Talent Review

training, coaching and experiences should be provided to aid each educator in reaching their potential.

Educators in boxes 1–3 should be stretched, developed and retained at all costs. Job shadowing, special projects and leadership roles are perfect for team members in these positions. Leveraging these educators to plan and deliver training to others is an excellent use of their talents, and a resource saving strategy for administrators. The next tier of educators, in boxes 5, 6 and 8, are core talent. Strategic talent leaders will not only work to retain these team members but will leverage resources to develop them through training and coaching. The lowest tier of performers are in boxes 4, 7 and 9. They are all underperformers. If employees in boxes 4 and 7 are willing to improve current practice, they can become core talent and even leaders. However, those in box 9 are not likely to improve unless significant resources are invested, at the expense of other employees. And yet, many principals prioritize educators in box 9, providing them all of their attention, coaches, training and resources, only to see them resign at the end of the school year or be coached out due to poor fit. The 9-Box Talent Review serves to present talent in nine boxes, forcing leaders to think about

Table 9.7 Action Steps for Evaluating

Best Practice	Data/Resources	Lead	Timeline

how to distribute resources across the evaluation spectrum to the benefit of improving student outcomes.

 # Action Steps for Evaluating

With your Talent Development Team, identify next steps in becoming more strategic in your evaluation practices.

- Which best practices are you already using to successfully evaluate talent?
- Which new practices would you like to begin implementing?
- In Table 9.7, list new practices for implementation, data/resources needed, a lead team member and the timeline for putting your next steps into action.

 # Talent Analytics for Evaluating

You have now assessed your current practices and identified some action steps. Below are the talent analytics, found in the Strategic Talent Leadership Scorecard (Appendix C), that you can use to measure and track your progress towards being a strategic talent leader.

1. The number and percentage of educators rated as 'ineffective' by school
2. The number and percentages of educator rating that overestimate or underestimate effectiveness

3. The number and percentages of educators retained, terminated and promoted by evaluation rating

4. The number and percentage of students at-risk assigned to under-performing and highly effective teachers

5. The number and percentage of highly effective teachers by licensure and degree granting college/university

Case Study Response

Now that you have learned more about best practices for evaluating educators, what advice would you give to Aanya and her principal, Ulises Rivera? Write your response in the space below:

_____

_____

_____

_____

_____

References

Bill and Melinda Gates Foundation. (2013). *Ensuring fair and reliable measures of effective teaching: Culminating findings from the met project's three-year study*. Bill & Melinda Gates Foundation. Retrieved from: https://k12education.gatesfoundation.org/download/?Num=2572&-filename=MET_Ensuring_Fair_and_Reliable_Measures_Practitioner_Brief.pdf

Cantrell, S. (2012). *Measuring effective teaching: A potential for change*. The Bill & Melinda Gates Foundation. Available online at: https://www.impatientoptimists.org/Posts/2012/01/Measuring-Effective-Teaching-A-Potential-for-Change?p=1

Haycock, K. 1998). Good teaching matters: How well-qualified teachers can close the gap. *Thinking K-16, 3*(2). Retrieved from http://search.ebscohost.com.libproxy.highpoint.edu/login.aspx?direct=true&db=eric&AN=ED457260&site=ehost-live

Hill, H., Herlihy, C., & American Enterprise Institute for Public Policy Research. (2011). *Prioritizing teaching quality in a new system of teacher evaluation. Education Outlook. No. 9.* American Enterprise Institute for Public Policy Research. Retrieved from: https://cepr.harvard.edu/files/cepr/files/ncte-prioritizing-teacher-quality-herlihy-hill.pdf

Mead, S., Rotherham, A., Brown, R., & American Enterprise Institute for Public Policy Research. (2012). *The hangover: Thinking about the unintended consequences of the nation's teacher evaluation binge.* American Enterprise Institute for Public Policy Research. Retrieved from https://bellwethereducation.org/sites/default/files/TeacherQuality_TheHangover_0.pdf

Rivers, J., & Sanders, W. (1996). *Cumulative and residual effects of teachers on future student academic achievement.* Knoxville, TN: University of Tennessee Value-Added Research and Assessment Center. Retrieved from: https://www.heartland.org/publications-resources/publications/cumulative-and-residual-effects-of-teachers-on-future-student-academic-achievement

The New Teacher Project. (2010). *Teacher evaluation 2.0.* Brooklyn, NY: TNTP. Retrieved from: https://tntp.org/publications/scroll/evaluation-and-development

US Department of Education. (2011). *ESEA Flexibility.* Washington, DC: US Department of Education. Retrieved from: www.ed.gov/esea/flexibility

Weisberg, D., Sexton, S., Mulhern, J., & Keeling, D. (2009). *The widget effect: Our national failure to acknowledge and act on differences in teacher effectiveness.* Brooklyn, NY: TNTP. Retrieved from: http://tntp.org/publications/reports/the-widget-effect/

Talent Assessment

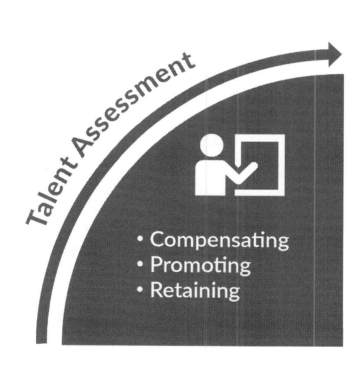

Compensating

Felicia Jeffries is a highly effective 5th-grade math teacher at a Title I elementary school. Year after year, her students achieve the highest growth in her school and some of the highest growth in the entire district. She is proud of her impact and does all that she can to mentor new teachers in her building to duplicate her results. Any time her principal asks her to sit on a committee, take charge of a project or organize the 5th-grade field trip, she enthusiastically says yes. Recently, the superintendent announced a program to recruit new STEM teachers to all 10 Title I elementary schools in the district. All newly hired STEM teachers would receive a $5,000 signing bonus and a $10,000 salary increase for as long as they remained at their schools. Unfortunately, as a current teacher, Felicia was not eligible for the bonus or salary increase. When asked by parents at her supper club what she thinks about the new compensation program, Felicia shared that it was a waste of taxpayer money.

Compensating Talent

Compensating is the practice of providing monetary and nonmonetary rewards to employees in exchange for time, effort and expertise. Monetary compensation is traditionally provided in the form of a salary, stipends, retirement and health benefits. Nonmonetary compensation can include leave days, attendance at conferences, opportunities to participate in activities, the provision of classroom supplies/resources and even preferential room assignments and class schedules. Ensuring that employees understand the full range and value of their compensation can be challenging. A well-explained and strategic compensation package can make recruiting and retention easy. For that reason, compensation is a key function of a strategic talent leadership approach.

Educator Compensation

For most of the 20th and 21st centuries, the American education system has used a compensation model made up of steps and lanes where the steps represented years of experience and the lanes, educational level or degree attainment. For example, Lane A might be for those with a bachelor's degree, Lane B, a master's degree and Lane C, a doctorate. Thus, if I am a teacher with a master's degree and 10 years of experience, my pay grade would be described as B-10. The strengths of this long-standing model are its clarity and perceived fairness. The system virtually eliminates pay previously differentiated by gender, race and age. Unfortunately, experience and degree attainment "have consistently failed to correlate with student outcomes leaving districts basing teacher pay on factors unrelated to performance in the classroom" (Podgursky & Springer, 2007). Annually, school districts across the nation spend $8.6 billion dollars to pay for advanced degrees that show no correlation or a negative correlation between degree status and student achievement outcomes (NCTQ, 2010).

In addition to the majority of school districts using a compensation model not connected to student outcomes, a disadvantage of the step and lane structure is that it significantly delays the age at which a teacher will realize his or her highest level of pay. In a 2010 study of teacher pay, researchers at the National Council on Teacher Quality (NCTQ) found that while doctors and lawyers reach peak earnings at ages 35 and 40, respectively, it takes a teacher 20–25 additional years of work to reach top earnings at 55. This is discouraging for highly effective educators who would be recognized as, and rewarded for, being top performers in their field regardless of age and experience. In their extensive review of teacher performance pay, Podgursky and Springer (2007) also discovered that since 1950, the percentage of school districts using this type of compensation model has only decreased by one percentage point from 97 down to 96 percent. And so, the federal government decided to incentivize states and local school districts to begin moving away from the step and lane system and begin thinking about how to connect teacher pay and student performance.

In 2005, the federal Department of Education created Teacher Incentive Fund grants, designed to support strategic talent leaders in designing differentiated teacher compensation programs. Just ten years later, a study by the Center for American Progress (Konoske-Graf, Partelow, & Benner, 2016) identified that one-third of districts were offering some form of pay incentive, increase or bonus. Twenty-five percent of districts were using these differentiated structures to incent recruitment, retention or both. Jonathan Eckert, National Institute for Excellence in Teaching, followed these trends as districts were shifting away from traditional salary models and beginning to adopt differentiated pay practices. Across the Teacher Incentive Fund grant sites (including one that I was leading), he identified six themes:

- Theme 1: Performance compensation is most effective when integrated with professional development, collaboration and evaluation as a comprehensive approach to system-wide improvement.

- Theme 2: Wide stakeholder involvement is essential to the design, implementation and effectiveness of compensation reform efforts.

- Theme 3: Financial incentives reward additional work and success, but they are valued as a component of a broader emphasis on improving teaching and learning.

- Theme 4: Nearly all of the sites created teacher leader positions with significant additional compensation to provide school-based support, evaluation and oversight for instructional improvement.

- Theme 5: Success in implementing these challenging reforms with fidelity is enhanced when states and districts provide staff positions, offer programmatic support and tie local efforts to state policies and funding.

- Theme 6: Financial sustainability is enhanced when state and district funds are reallocated to support performance compensation reforms (Eckert, 2013).

What Eckert recognized, and what we all learned, is that educator pay is not a stand-alone solution for improving student outcomes. It must play a critical role within an aligned strategic talent leadership framework. The pay

Table 10.1 Strategic Talent Leadership Insights for Compensating

Strategic Practice	Yes	Not Yet
Our organization ensures that educator base salaries (without additional incentives) are equitable across Title I and non-Title I schools.		
Our organization's educator compensation plan includes monetary and nonmonetary rewards.		
Our organization's compensation plan is structured to be responsive to market demands.		
Our organization's compensation plan is designed to achieve locally identified talent goals.		
Our organization's compensation plan is accurately understood by current and potential employees.		

structure must support recruitment and retention. But, it must also be aligned to and in support of robust evaluation systems, professional development that is responsive to evaluation results, coaching and mentoring that help in increasing educator effectiveness. And, all of that must be situated within working conditions that are conducive to both educator and student success.

 # Strategic Talent Leadership Insights for Compensating

With your Strategic Talent Leadership Team, review the strategic talent leadership practices for compensating (see Table 10.1). If you are currently engaging in a practice, check 'yes.' If not, check 'not yet' and consider how this practice could be adopted by your organization as you read through the best practices described in this chapter.

 # Best Practices for Compensating

Ensure Pay Equity across Schools

Across the nation, there are hidden pay inequities between Title I and non-Title I schools. As a best practice for compensating educators, this should be regularly analyzed and addressed. Teachers who work at Title I schools, the nation's hardest-to-staff schools, tend to be younger and have less experience (Carver-Thomas & Darling-Hammond, 2017). And, because most of our districts still use a traditional step and lane pay schedule, this translates into 'cheaper.' By way of years of experience, the average salary of a teacher at a Title I school tends to be less that at non-Title I schools. Therefore, districts are making a greater talent investment in non-Title I schools that are staffed with 'more expensive' teachers, giving further advantage to those schools that already educate populations of students that come from homes with greater monetary resources.

While still working in a large, urban school district, I collaborated with our team to pull all teacher salaries across the district in an effort to highlight this hidden inequity. We sorted all salaries into two categories—those that were teachers at Title I schools and those that were not. Our predictions were correct! The average salary at our Title I schools was $47,000, while the non-Title I schools averaged $54,000 (Table 10.2). At the level of a singular teacher, this $7,000 pay difference may not seem significant. But, when you compound it at the school-wide level, the inequity it creates is criminal.

When comparing Title I and non-Title I schools of similar sizes, there are significant differences in the human capital investments between the two school types that favor *non*-Title I schools. But, not to worry, federal Title I dollars mitigate these differences … right? Wrong. Let's estimate that each of the 500 students at Title I School A yields the school $600 per

Table 10.2 Sample Title I versus Non-Title I School Salary Comparison

School	Average Salary	Number of Teachers	Salary Investment
Title I School A	$47,000	50	$2,350,000
Non-Title I School A	$54,000	50	$2,700,000
Title I School Talent Investment Disadvantage			**($350,000)**
Title I School B	$47,000	100	$4,700,000
Non-Title I School B	$54,000	100	$5,400,000
Title I School Talent Investment Disadvantage			**($700,000)**
Title I School C	$47,000	150	$7,050,000
Non-Title I School C	$54,000	150	$8,100,000
Title I School Talent Investment Disadvantage			**($1,050,000)**

Table 10.3 Sample Funding Gap between Title I and Non-Title I Schools

School	Title I School Talent Investment Disadvantage	Title I Funding ($600 per child)	Remaining Gap
Title I School A	$350,000	$300,000	$50,000
Title I School B	$700,000	$600,000	$100,000
Title I School C	$1,050,000	$900,000	$150,000

year in federal funds. That would bring the total amount of federal Title I dollars allocated to the school to $300,000 annually. I'm sure you've already figured out that the 'supplemental' Title I dollars are $50,000 less that the salary advantage already present in the non-Title I school (Table 10.3). Thus, the supplemental funds that are meant to give Title I schools an advantage fail to help the school achieve *equal* resources, let alone a needed advantage.

There are many ways to counteract this inequity. Districts can be allocated teacher funding at the rate of the 'average district teacher salary' per full-time equivalent (FTE) position and require principals to staff according to their available funds (this has inherent issues in that principals may discriminate against more experienced, and expensive, teachers). School districts can also leverage strategic staffing, weighted student funding formulas that eliminate the funding disadvantage, or consider developing compensation plans designed to motivate teachers to self-select placement in hard-to-staff schools and positions. The purpose of highlighting this best practice is not to offer a resolution, which is an individual district decision, rather, to call attention to the importance of recognizing whether or not this inequity exists in your organization.

Diversify Compensation with Monetary and Nonmonetary Rewards

Money isn't everything. Or, at least that is what annual Gallup, PDK and MetLife surveys of teachers tell us. In addition to pay, working conditions, professional development, opportunities for advancement and access to administrative support are cited as reasons that teachers choose to remain in the profession. In creating a strategic compensation plan that is effective in recruiting and retaining top talent, we need to expand our thinking beyond monetary compensation and consider other rewards. Traditional monetary compensation can include salary, stipends, paid benefits and paid retirement contributions. These represent a direct transfer of dollars to an employee, whether into their bank account or retirement account.

Rewards provided to educators that are not a direct transfer of dollars (nonmonetary) can be further broken down into two categories—(a) nonmonetary rewards that have a monetary cost to the district and (b) nonmonetary rewards that have no monetary cost to the district. Examples of the first category include the district paying the cost for an educator to go back to school to earn a master's or doctoral degree, covering the cost of conference attendance and even paying for the testing fees to add additional licensure areas. While these are nonmonetary rewards for the educator, they do come with a price tag for the organization. In contrast, districts can provide nonmonetary rewards to educators that have no tangible cost. Examples include:

- Changes in job title (from teacher to teacher leader or assistant principal to dean of students)
- Electronic badges that can be included in an email signature, designating specialized expertise, advanced skills or leadership roles
- Opportunities to serve in leadership roles or to have greater representation within the school leadership structure
- Release time in exchange for performing extra duties
- Preferred classroom placement
- Access to additional teaching resources and technology

Each of the above examples carries value to educators that is nonmonetary. And, each is a method of rewarding an educator for the time and effort they are dedicating to the organization. Occasionally, I would email my staff that because we achieved XYZ goal, everyone could leave 15 minutes early on a Friday afternoon. Based upon the cheers that erupted upon receipt of the email, you would think that I just handed out $1,000 bonus checks. Do not ever underestimate the value of a small thank you. A 'Friday Jeans Day' can surprisingly get you a lot of traction! Key to crafting a compensation plan is identifying what is valued by the educators in your organization and formalizing how these are awarded in order to maximize recruitment and retention benefits.

Respond to Market Trends

Traditional step and lane compensation systems have made it difficult for schools to be responsive to market trends in the way that corporate employers can be (Goldhaber, 2010). The upside is that they are very easy to understand. When a principal in a district with a step and lane pay system identifies a top candidate, she/he can only offer the candidate the promise of better working conditions, a preferred course load, reduced extra duties, etc., but not additional pay as a means of motivating the candidate to accept the position. For principals of highly impacted schools, it's a tough sell. Even when school districts *have* been able to incorporate differentiated pay into their compensation system, it tends to look like a layered cake with the 'old' pay scale serving as the foundational layer and additional layers stacked on top, funded with additional dollars (Figure 10.1). Oftentimes, those additional dollars are grant funded or are discretionary dollars that are the first to get cut in a budget crisis.

Ideally, districts would fully redesign compensation systems based upon sustainable funding, paying attention to factors such as teacher effectiveness, hard-to-staff positions, hard-to-staff schools, course loads and leadership duties. "Truly effective teacher pay reform is best achieved by aligning compensation with a district's primary needs: improving student achievement and placing the best teachers where they are needed most" (NCTQ, 2010, p. 1). But, transitioning your entire pay system from Plan A to Plan B can be a challenge. Organizations such as the District of Columbia and Denver Public Schools effectively ran two pay plans in

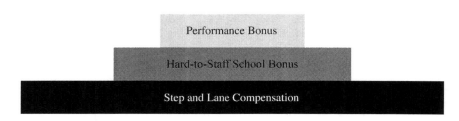

Figure 10.1 Sample Differentiated Pay System

parallel in order to grandfather in educators who wanted to stay on the 'old' compensation model while requiring that any new hires be placed on the 'new' compensation model. Teachers are largely in favor of pay reform (Goldhaber, DeArmond, & DeBurgomaster, 2007) when additional pay is linked to serving in hard-to-staff positions and schools. Leveraged strategically, differentiated compensation can yield more equitable distribution of teacher talent within and across schools by making it easier for principals to recruit and retain highly effective educators.

Align Compensation to District and School Talent Goals

When Felicia Jeffries first learned about her district's new compensation plan, her immediate reaction was anger. In fact, she shared with parents that the plan was a waste of taxpayer money. She was a top performer who had dedicated herself to her students and school, rejecting offers to leave and teach at 'easier schools' year after year. Her reward ... the opportunity to watch brand new teachers come on board and make $15,000 more than she. This was a plan that was NOT aligned to achieve her district's talent goals. In fact, the compensation plan, designed without teacher input, could be a mitigating factor in Felicia deciding to leave her current school. In my experience leading a locally funded teacher compensation model and two federal Teacher Incentive Fund grant programs, the most important factor for success is that the program be locally designed with teacher input and responsive to local talent needs. If the district's greatest need is recruiting teachers, an emphasis should be put on offering recruitment incentives. This is a challenge shared nationally by rural districts who have a more difficult time attracting younger, recent college graduates, to move to areas with fewer social activities. In contrast, a large urban district might be attractive to younger teachers seeking a wide variety of social activities. However, the urban district might be challenged to retain teachers due to the emotional impacts of supporting students living in extreme poverty and trauma. A locally designed program in this district would emphasize retention incentives. While these two examples are gross stereotypes, they exemplify that each district is unique in its needs and, therefore, should have a fully customized compensation program that is tightly aligned with the talent goals and outcomes of the district.

Once developed, it is critical that educators be able to trust that the compensation model will be sustained. If a district is enticing an educator to leave his or her school and transfer to a hard-to-staff school with the promise of pay incentives, that educator must trust that the compensation plan will be in place long-term. I once worked with a school board that voted in May on funding for the upcoming school year where pay incentives were a part of the district's overall budget. Despite numerous conversations, board members failed to understand that the recruiting season ran January thru April and that incentives voted on *after* the recruiting season ended could not be leveraged *during* the recruiting season! They also failed to recognize that educators will not leave ideal working conditions for more challenging assignments if the pay incentives to do so are subject to annual approval. In order to build trust and confidence in the compensation system, organizations must be able to ensure sustainability over time.

Additional guidelines for developing and implementing locally responsive compensation models include best practices identified by Heneman, Milanowski, and Kimball (2007) in a synthesis of compensation plans from across the United States. They recommend that organizations:

- guarantee stable and adequate funding;
- provide competitive total compensation;
- build strong measurement systems (to track teacher performance); and
- gauge likely teacher reactions to the performance pay plan (not necessary if teachers are engaged in the planning process from the start).

Later in this chapter, Strategic Talent Leadership Tool 10—Differentiated Compensation Planner, is offered as a tool for districts and schools to use in identifying types of compensation and aligning each of the incentives to a strategic talent outcome. Once the input and design process is completed, the next best practice in communicating how the plan works.

Communicate the Total Compensation Plan Value

The more complex your compensation plan, the more you will have to communicate about it in order for educators to fully understand it. The best design strategy is one that can be encapsulated into an elevator speech and understood with 100 percent accuracy. Educators who sign on to a differentiated compensation plan must not only be able to trust that it will be in place long-term, they must trust that the compensation structure explained to them is the one that will be implemented and, ultimately, show up in their paycheck. The best way to build this trust is to ensure that all principals, teachers and compensation plan administrators have the same understanding of the 'rules.' This can be easily accomplished by created a memorandum of understanding or a contract that outlines:

- the compensation plan and incentives;
- requirements for incentive eligibility;
- disqualifications for incentive eligibility; and
- a process for appealing any incentive payments or nonpayments.

In leading North Carolina's longest running differentiated compensation plan, my team learned that we had to refine our educator contract each year based upon lessons learned. For example, we were once challenged by a teacher who claimed that *if she had generated a Value-Added Data report,* she would have qualified for the $10,000 performance incentive. As a result, we had to add "you must be teaching courses for which you generate a Value-Added Data Teacher Index report in order to qualify for the Value-Added Data Teacher Index performance incentive" to the fine print of our contract. Don't ever assume what is intuitively obvious to most is obvious to all!

Strategies for communicating your differentiated compensation plan, in addition to asking educators to sign annual contracts, include:

- Create a compensation program brochure that outlines the incentive model, requirements to qualify for each incentive, disqualifiers (for example … getting fired) and the process for appeals.
- Include overviews of your compensation program in all recruitment materials. And, educate your recruiters and principals (often one in the same) so that they can well explain the program.
- Create a compensation program website, rich with information, data and examples. Include a frequently asked questions page

where you log all questions you receive over time and the answers to them. This will also ensure internal consistency in program implementation.

- Host annual information sessions at each school in which the compensation program is in place.
- Create compensation program ambassadors at each school who are trained experts in your program that can answer questions on site. A lead teacher or educator who was involved in the development of the program is an ideal choice.
- Conduct an annual survey to determine principal, teacher and program administrator levels of understanding about the compensation incentives, requirements and disqualifications.

At the program administration level, be sure to designate someone who is charged with managing the compensation program and conducting annual program evaluations to determine its effectiveness. This person should regularly provide reports to senior leadership, board members and principals about the impacts of the program on strategic talent goals. Over communication about the program on the front end, evaluation of the program's goals and celebrations of its impacts will help to ensure that the return on your compensation program investment shows up as improved student outcomes.

Strategic Talent Leadership Tool 10— Differentiated Compensation Planner

What would Felicia Jeffries's ideal compensation program look like? Would it include a performance incentive for math teachers who, like her, consistently generate 1.5+ years of growth in one school year? Would it include a retention bonus for staying at a hard-to-staff school? What about an incentive for her perfect attendance? The people who best know what incentives should be designed into a compensation program are those that you want to incent! The very first step you should take when designing a new compensation program is to form a representative group of those who will lead the program, leverage the program in recruiting and hiring and those who will be beneficiaries of the program. Once identified, your team should commit to working through a multistep process of:

- understanding the organization's current compensation program, its pros and cons;
- understanding the compensation landscape of education across the country, including the varied models being used and their impacts;
- becoming knowledgeable of the organization's talent needs and goals (where are there shortages, what is hard to staff, where is their high turnover, etc.);
- being informed about the available funding for a compensation program; and
- understanding any policy or practice parameters that will be applied to the program.

Resourced with this information, the team will be prepared to begin the discussions about possibilities. In leading many such teams, one of my ice-breaker activities was to pass out a Hershey Bar to each team member. This plain chocolate bar is scored into 12 smaller pieces, allowing the bar to be easily broken apart and shared. I challenge team members to imagine that the entire bar represents the total incentives available to them in designing a new compensation plan and ask that they break up the bar and assign the 12 pieces to a defined group for a defined outcome. What happens next perfectly exemplifies the complexity of creating an effective compensation program. Recommended chocolate incentive plans either fail to achieve any strategic outcome because the team members decided to distribute the pieces evenly (also known as a raise ... not differentiated compensation), or they realized that they could not achieve all of their outcomes because they didn't have enough chocolate to do so. Once the 'ah-ha' occurs and team members understand the concept of differentiation and the tension between achieving goals and leveraging resources, the real conversations can begin. As a next step, strategic talent leaders can ask planning team members to use the Compensation Cost and Impact Analysis chart in Table 10.4. On the x-axis is impact and on the y-axis, cost. In each cell is a description of high/low cost or high/low impact. Team members should begin to populate the chart with monetary and nonmonetary forms of compensation available within the organization. For example, offering a

Table 10.4 Compensation Cost and Impact Analysis

Cost	+	High Cost Low Impact	High Cost High Impact
	−	Low Cost Low Impact	Low Cost High Impact
		−	+
	Impact		

$2,500 sign-on bonus for STEM teachers who sign an early contract might be a high-cost-high-impact strategy. But, offering 'trade days' to teachers who lead evening and weekend events might be a low-cost-high-impact strategy. This brainstorming activity will result in generating a robust list of possible compensation strategies that can be incorporated into your final program design.

With compensation strategies in hand, team members can begin defining the outcomes that could be aligned to the strategies identified. At this point, the team is not yet asked to finalize the program design, merely to generate the alignment between the strategy, the cost, the targeted audience and the desired talent outcome. The purpose of this activity is to help team members think through the 'why' of each type of compensation. This will eventually help in narrowing down which strategies are of most valuable in achieving overall talent outcomes (Table 10.5).

The final design phase of creating a differentiated compensation plan includes creating a model that takes the selected compensation strategies, projects out the number of educators who will qualify for the incentive and calculates the total cost. The model can then be adjusted to increase or decrease incentive amounts, target audiences and projected outcomes until the total cost is within budget. For example, a model might project that 50 math teachers each receive a performance incentive of $10,000 for a total cost of $500,000. But, if the budget only allows for $300,000, the incentive will either have to be reduced to $6,000 or the threshold raised to reduce the number of qualifiers to 30. Surprisingly, the modeling is the easy part because you will likely have a budget that needs to be met. Once your model meets budget, you are now ready to share your differentiated compensation program with a broader audience for the purpose of seeking feedback before finalizing the program design.

Table 10.5 Sample Compensation Alignment to Outcomes

Compensation Type	Cost per Person	Audience	Targeted Outcome
Early contract signing bonus	$2,500	STEM teachers	Achieve 100% staffing of STEM teachers on the first day of school
Hard to staff position bonus	$5,000	STEM teachers working in any school	Retain STEM teachers across the district
Hard to staff position bonus	$4,000	EC teachers in Title I Schools	Retain EC teachers in high-need schools
Performance bonus	$10,000	STEM teachers in Title I Schools	Recruit and retain high-performing STEM teachers in high-need schools
Attendance bonus	$1,000	Teachers with 100% attendance	Reduce the number of days students are taught by a substitute
1 Course release	.25 FTE	Beginning teachers	Increase beginning teacher retention by providing extra planning and support time
5-Year extended contract	$0	Highly effective teachers	Retain highly effective teachers through the provision of additional job security

Table 10.6 Action Steps for Compensating

Best Practice	Required Resources	Lead	Timeline

 # Action Steps for Compensating

With your Talent Development Team, identify next steps in becoming more strategic in your compensating practices.

- Which best practices are you already using to successfully compensate educators?
- Which new practices would you like to begin implementing?
- Table 10.6 lists new practices for implementation, data/resources needed, a lead team member and the timeline for putting your next steps into action.

 # Talent Analytics for Compensating

You have now assessed your current practices and identified some action steps. Below are the talent analytics, found in the Strategic Talent Leadership Scorecard (Appendix C), that you can use to measure and track your progress toward being a strategic talent leader.

1. Average salaries by school type (Title I and Non-Title I)
2. Average salaries by teacher effectiveness levels
3. Average salaries by staffing difficulty (at the position and school levels)
4. Educators, by school who qualify for additional incentives
5. Percentages of current and future employees who accurately understand the compensation plan

Case Study Response

Now that you have learned more about best practices for compensating educators, what advice would you give to Felicia's school district? Write your response in the space below:

_____

_____

_____

_____

_____

References

Carver-Thomas, D., & Darling-Hammond, L. (2017). *Teacher turnover: Why it matters and what we can do about it.* Palo Alto, CA: Learning Policy Institute. Retrieved from: https://learningpolicyinstitute.org/sites/default/files/product-files/Teacher_Turnover_REPORT.pdf

Eckert, J. (2013). *Increasing educator effectiveness: Lessons learned from teacher incentive fund sites.* Nashville, TN: National Institute for Excellence in Teaching.

Goldhaber, D. (2010). *Teacher pay reforms: The political implications of recent research.* Seattle, WA: Center for Education Data and Research. Retrieved from: http://cedr.us/papers/working/CEDR%20WP%202010-4_Teacher%20Pay%20Reforms%20(8-23-10).pdf

Goldhaber, D., DeArmond, M. M., & DeBurgomaster, S. (2007). *Teacher attitudes about compensation reform: Implications for reform implementation.* SFRP Working Paper 20. Seattle WA. Center on Reinventing Public Education. Retrieved from: https://www.crpe.org/sites/default/files/wp_sfrp20_goldhaber_aug07_0.pdf

Heneman, H. G., Milanowski, A., & Kimball, S. (2007). *Teacher performance pay: Synthesis of plans, research, and guidelines for practice.* CPRE Policy Briefs, RB-46. Philadelphia, PA: Consortium for Policy Research in Education. Retrieved from: https://files.eric.ed.gov/fulltext/ED498341.pdf

Konoske-Graf, A., Partelow, L., & Benner, M. (2016). *To attract great teachers, school districts must improve their human capital systems.* Washington, DC: The Center for American Progress. Retrieved from: https://www.americanprogress.org/issues/education-k-12/reports/2016/12/22/295574/to-attract-great-teachers-school-districts-must-improve-their-human-capital-systems/

National Council on Teacher Quality (NCTQ). (2010). *Restructuring teacher pay to reward excellence.* Washington, DC: Author. Retrieved from: https://files.eric.ed.gov/fulltext/ED521227.pdf

Podgursky, M. J., & Springer, M. G. (2007). Teacher performance pay: A review. *Journal of Policy Analysis and Management, 26*(4), pp. 909–949.

Promoting

Tina Sonricker had been a principal for six years. Every two years, the super-intendent moved her to a different school, determined to find the right fit. Her colleagues all suspected that these moves had something to do with her lack of effectiveness as she never seemed to know what was going on during principal meetings. The superintendent was in a bind. Tina continued to get poor results but was well liked by community members and one school board member. She had to get her out of the principalship but knew that politically, she couldn't afford to demote her. When a central office role became vacant, she used it to her advantage and moved Sonricker immediately. Within hours, the other principals had heard the news and were already complaining that the best way to get promoted in the district was to underperform in your current role.

Promoting Talent

Promoting is the practice of increasing the scope of responsibilities and influence of an employee. A promotion is almost always accompanied by a new job title and may or may not include an increase in compensation. Promotions place an employee back at the start of the Strategic Talent Leadership cycle, requiring onboarding into the new position, induction throughout the first months and/or years, additional training, coaching and support. A primary strategy for engaging and retaining your top-performing employees, promoting is an important function within a strategic talent leadership approach.

At any given time, 25 percent of employees are actively seeking a promotion (Burgess, 2016). That is great news for organizations that are heavily investing in engaging their employees in training and development opportunities with the intention that they will remain in the organization and move up the proverbial ladder. But, this same research found that *not* receiving a promotion is cited by 24 percent of employees as the reason they look outside of their organization for employment. For that reason, it is critical to have a promotion strategy that is not only robust, but transparent, invoking trust and continued employee engagement. A strong talent management strategy will ensure that all employees, regardless of promotion attainment, remain engaged and valued in their role. Unfortunately, 95 percent of executives do not feel that their organizations are effectively managing talent (Andrianova, Maor, & Schaninger, 2018). This is also true of principals. As referenced earlier in the book, most principal preparation programs include one course in human resources with only a portion of that training addressing talent development. So, while principals might be great instructional leaders, they are not always the strongest leaders of talent. One key strategy that principals and district leaders alike can embrace is ensuring that all employees have access to career pathways that keep them engaged and retained within the organization. Smith (2012) has identified three key questions to ask in considering whether or not you, as a leader, are effectively providing your team with career pathways that lead to promotions:

- Are there real career opportunities available?
- Are they visible to your talent pool?
- Are there support structures that facilitate internal career moves?

These questions are applicable to providing promotion opportunities from baseline jobs all the way to the most senior level positions. While we tend to think of existing leaders seeking promotions, research tells us that even beginning teachers have the desire to take on greater levels of responsibility. Meyer and Lenarz (2019) have worked extensively with beginning teachers and have found that when they are provided with "opportunities to lead, they revitalize the school, enhance the professional community, and build meaningful careers." This chapter contains best practices to help

Table 11.1 Strategic Talent Leadership Insights for Promoting

Strategic Practice	Yes	Not Yet
Our organization assigns annual risk ratings to all critical leadership positions.		
Our organization has three or more potential successors identified for each critical leadership position.		
Our organization has clear and communicated processes for seeking promotions.		
Our organization uses pre-promotion strategies to upskill employees for future roles.		
Our organization offers career coaching opportunities to all employees.		

principals and district leaders hone in on best practices for facilitating promotions as well as tools for guiding educators, at all levels, through maximizing their career goals.

Strategic Talent Leadership Insights for Promoting

With your Strategic Talent Leadership Team, review the strategic talent leadership practices for promoting (see Table 11.1). If you are currently engaging in a practice, check 'yes.' If not, check 'not yet' and consider how this practice could be adopted by your organization as you read through the best practices described in this chapter.

Best Practices for Promoting Talent

Conduct Annual Risk Ratings

When news of a resignation causes panic throughout the school district, that is a sure sign that it was a critical leadership position. When leaders in key roles leave, the impact can be devastating, causing anxiety throughout the organization as team members speculate as to how the work will get done, who will fill the vacancy and what changes will occur as a result of the transition. But, the story does not have to play out in this manner. Key leadership transitions should not be surprises if an organization is conducting annual risk ratings. Risk ratings are exactly what they sound like—an assessment of the risk that a key leader will leave his or her role in the next six months. The purpose of conducting annual risk ratings is to predict and proactively prepare for potential transitions in an organization. For example, if the Chief Finance Officer of a school district has accumulated the 30 years required for retirement, is 65 years of age and has been talking about wanting to spend time with her new twin grandchildren, you probably have a 'high flight risk' on your hands! On the other hand of the spectrum, if you just hired a new Chief Academic Officer from out of state at a salary 30 percent higher than what he was previously making, paid for him to move his spouse and three young children into your district, helped to enroll them in the preferred elementary school, and he is telling everyone he's never been happier, he is likely going to be considered a 'low flight risk.'

The first step in conducting annual risk ratings is to identify a comprehensive list of roles that would negatively impact the organization if the current team member left. These roles will be different in each organization, but some typical key leadership roles may include:

- Superintendent
- Board of Education Attorney
- Chief Human Resources Officer
- Chief Finance Officer
- Chief Academic Officer
- Chief Operations Officer
- Principal Supervisors
- Principals
- Director of Technology (or any role requiring highly technical expertise)
- Director of Special Education

Once these roles have been identified, the next step is for a knowledgeable team, that likely includes many of these team members, to assess the likelihood of the leader leaving within the next six months. Ratings can easily be grouped into three categories—(a) high flight risk, (b) moderate flight risk and (c) low flight risk. Factors that can influence the risk rating assigned to each critical team member include but are not limited to:

- retirement eligibility and partner/spouse's retirement eligibility;
- age and partner/spouse's age;
- health;
- family responsibilities (especially taking care of elderly family members);
- current compensation level;
- other job opportunities (especially soon after another key team member leaves and might be trying to recruit trusted colleagues to join him/her in the new organization);
- working conditions and job satisfaction; and
- opportunities to move up in the organization.

These are certainly not all of the influencing factors but they are a starting place for thinking about what would motivate a key team member to stay or go. Above all of these, the best indicator is listening to what the employee is saying about their career intentions. While this can be achieved informally, Chapter 12 will introduce a tool that can be used to gather information that can help to inform risk ratings.

Engage in Succession Planning

Succession planning is the cyclical process of recruiting leaders, retaining them and simultaneously planning for their replacement should they leave. It is widely underutilized in the field of education and yet it is "one avenue to address leadership issues and help school district leaders meet their long-term leadership needs" (Cieminski, 2018, p. 21). The best succession plans identify key leadership roles, highly qualified replacements for those leaders and provide the upskilling necessary to ensure that the replacements experience minimal transition barriers when they assume positions of greater responsibility (Parfitt, 2017).

Specifically, organizations that engage in succession planning identify candidates for future leadership roles and provide them with individualized professional development, job shadowing experiences, coaching and job counseling. The process itself is a strategy to increase employee engagement and retention. When team members can visualize a future in an organization, they are more likely to remain in that organization that is investing in their future. Rothwell (2005) has identified several key characteristics of effective succession planning. For educational organization, they include:

- personnel dedicated to leading, being accountable for and communicating the succession planning process;
- participation of senior leaders in the identification of future leaders;
- use of benchmarks and needs assessments to determine readiness;
- emphasis on succession planning at all school and district leadership levels;
- identification of time frames for high-level replacements;
- having accountability to prepare one's own successors; and
- specific training and development opportunities, including formal mentoring, provided to future leaders.

While there are robust software tools available to manage all HR functions, including succession planning, low-tech approaches can work as well. For example, a simple spreadsheet or database documenting key leadership roles, risk ratings and potential successors could be sufficient for schools or small districts (Table 11.2).

Using your succession planning database will help you to identify key team members who need targeted training and development. This will ensure that you are creating a "a dynamic process that simultaneously includes forecasting upcoming openings and preparing a pipeline of qualified individuals…enabling the gains made by one leader to be sustained in spite of the transition" (Peters-Hawkins, Reed, & Kingsberry, 2018, p. 54). For example, Kathy Cawley will likely be a candidate to replace Donna Lloyd, current Chief Human Resources Officer, within the next six months. Knowing this, Kathy can be provided opportunities to begin taking over some of Donna's duties, shadowing Donna at cabinet and board meetings,

Table 11.2 Sample Succession Planning Database

Key Leadership Role	Current	Risk Rating	Potential 1	Potential 2	Potential 3
Chief Human Resources Officer	Donna Lloyd	High	Kathy Cawley, Executive Director of HR	Felicia Chavis, Director of HR	Shelena Bowser, Executive Director of Counseling
Chief Finance Officer	Casey Martin	Low	Tammy Brady, Director of Procurement	Wynde Taylor, Executive Director of Payroll	Debbie Hopkins, Director of Finance
Northern High School Principal	Ben Bowie	Moderate	Natalie Smith, Assistant Principal of Northern Elementary	Terrik Landreth, Principal of Southern Elementary	Michelle Higgins, Director of Title I

learning about required state and federal reporting and even register for a new HR director academy offered by a national professional organization. That type of proactive planning can help to mitigate potential transition issues and can shorten Kathy's time to full productivity once hired. Should Kathy not be interested in the role or not be chosen for the role, the other two high-potential successors should also be fielded opportunities for upskilling for this or other roles.

Communicate Promotion Opportunities

In a scan of hundreds of school websites, the one consistency was a lack of consistency in promoting employment opportunities. The strongest organizational websites had clearly designated links to find employment opportunities, while the very worst required seven clicks to reach job listings. While it takes 364 licks to get to the center of a Tootsie Pop, it should only take one click to get to your employment opportunities! Accessibility to job information is key but, once it's found, potential candidates must trust that a job posting is accurate and that the vacancies are true. Organizations sometimes post job openings for the purpose of resume gathering in the case of an eventual opening. While this is not illegal, it is misleading and creates trust issues with potential job candidates. Additionally, some organizations are known for posting jobs for which candidates have already been hired in order to meet board of education requirements. In advertising job opportunities, transparency is by far the best approach for not only attracting the best candidates but retaining them. This is especially critical for maintaining trust among current employees seeing promotions. Consider building internal and external trust by:

- creating a vision statement that explains that your organization's hiring priorities (diversity priorities, internal vs external hiring ratios, promotion from within, etc.);

- as a courtesy to current employees, send out an email notification of vacancies to internal candidates prior to publicly posting opportunities for external candidates;

- be clear with internal candidates that while you value current employees, external candidates often have fresh perspectives, different experiences and can be natural facilitators growth (Sabina & Colwell, 2018);

- post hiring procedures on your human resources website so that they are readily viewable even if they are also posted in your board of education policies and procedures

- post all job descriptions and salary schedules on your human resources website so that they are accessible to candidates; and

- as a part of your annual working conditions survey, be sure to ask employees if they know how to seek out and secure promotions.

Promoting from within is a strategic retention strategy. When current employees see colleagues being given opportunities to increase their scope, influence and pay, they trust that they, too, have access to promotions. This belief increases the value employees feel toward their organization which, in turn, increases their retention within the organization.

Leverage Pre-Promotion Activities

Strategic talent leaders not only identify key leadership positions for risk ratings, seek out and name potential successors and clearly communicate promotion opportunities, they proactively facilitate pre-promotion activities. Replacing a key leadership position requires both an investment of time and monetary resources. Where better to spend those resources than on the high-potential successors to those positions? Sometimes called 'stretch' programs, organizations that upskill employees for future roles are getting double the return on their investment—instead of using one pot of money to recruit and another to train and develop candidates, they are leveraging funds to grow their own future leaders for internal promotions. Some of these activities include:

- student teacher academies;
- teacher leadership academies;
- aspiring leadership academies;
- job shadowing and job rotations;
- cross-training and job sharing;

- coaching and career counseling; and
- job overlapping to give a newly promoted candidate time to learn from the outgoing candidate.

Strategically, it is better to invest recruitment and hiring dollars in developing upskilling programs to prepare current employees for hard-to-staff roles and leave remaining recruiting dollars for use in hiring for easier to fill positions. If possible, track pre-promotion activities in your succession planning database and align them with the skills, knowledge and aptitudes necessary for success in the future role.

Offer Career Coaching

I am a huge fan of Michael Bungay Stanier. He presents each year at the International Association for Talent Development conference and I don't ever miss his sessions. One year, he announced his death date to the audience. We all sat up a little and leaned in to hear what was next. What he explained next made more sense to me than any career advice or coaching book I had ever read. He said that knowing the date of your death will change how you work forever. Stanier proceeded to explain that most people are able to achieve one major accomplishment every five years. Theoretically, if you had 35 years until your 'death date,' you could plan to achieve seven major accomplishments, 25 years, five accomplishments and so on. While we obviously cannot pinpoint our actual date of death, the importance of this awareness comes into play when thinking about our career goals. No matter what term your organization uses to describe getting from where you are now to where you want to be (ladders, lattices, pathways), there are two considerations to be taken—your projected active work years and the qualifications that will enable your eligibility for future roles.

If it is your desire to plan out your future active work years, it can be helpful to have a career coach with whom you can discuss viable opportunities. Career coaches usually have knowledge of job roles and key insights about opportunities not necessarily available to the lay worker. For example, a teacher may only think that his/her future opportunities are to be an Assistant Principal and then a Principal because that is the model that is visible on a daily basis. Meeting with a career coach might illuminate other opportunities such as instructional coach, Title I specialist, school psychologist, international student enrollment counselor, etc. Career coaching conversations can be mutually beneficial. Employees learn about opportunities that align with their future goals and employers have the opportunity to educate team members about upcoming workforce needs. Ideally, every organization would have a role, or roles, in human resources that have the ability to sit down with employees and facilitate career planning discussions. At school sites, principals are excellent sources of career coaching because they are already having discussions with educators about performance. The addition of future opportunities to evaluation conversations is a natural one. In support of these conversations is Strategic Talent Leadership Tool 11. Guided Pathways are maps to help inform educators about the knowledge, skills and aptitudes necessary to be eligible for key roles within an organization. Resourced with Guided Pathways, career coaches and principals can provide appropriate guidance to educators wanting to grow professionally within an organization.

Strategic Talent Leadership Tool 11— Guided Pathways

If our case study principal, Tina Sonricker, had the opportunity to meet with a career coach, she may have realized that her current skill set was not well aligned to the principalship. A strong career coach would have discussed with her that she still had 15 years remaining until she qualified for retirement from the organization, enough time to obtain her school psychologist license, enabling her the ability to work one-on-one with students, their teachers and families. This was the very part of the principalship that Tina loved the most … not the instructional supervision, hiring or budgeting. She wanted to spend time problem-solving individual student cases to ensure that each child received equitable opportunities to grow. Instead, she was being moved around the district as if on a carousel and being talked about by her peers. Her greatest desire was to add value to the organization and feel great about her accomplishments.

Results from a 2015 Career Frameworks survey (Mercer) found that globally, half of all talent management organizations use career frameworks to help employees identify 'right fit' jobs within their organizations. Career frameworks are systems that include standardized job descriptions, pre-identified job qualifications and aligned development opportunities. Similar to succession planning, more widely used in corporate settings, career frameworks are not broadly used in education. The use of these frameworks, or any guided pathway to a future role, is in strong alignment with strategic talent leadership efforts. Guided Pathways provide school districts a standardized tool for communicating the skills, knowledge and aptitudes required for qualified job candidacy.

Schools and districts wanting to adopt Guided Pathways should first create a list of positions for which a pathway makes sense. Typically, a position that represents a promotion from a baseline job is an ideal opportunity for the use of a pathway. Thus, most leadership positions would be a good starting place for the development of pathways. Once pathway positions are defined, individual Guided Pathways must be developed. The tool is structured around five distinct categories:

- Degrees and Professional Licensure
- Work Experiences
- Workshops and Training
- Activities and Experiences
- Academies and Certificates

These categories are meant to capture all of the qualifications that an ideal candidate for the job role would possess. The provided sample is for the role of a principal (Figure 11.1). In theory, a qualified candidate would have at least 100 points, distributed across the five categories, in order to be considered for the role of a principal. Candidates who exceed 100 points would exhibit more than the minimum requirements to be considered for candidacy.

It is recommended that the designers of each Guided Pathway be personnel currently serving in the role. For our sample pathway, the HR director and a group of four to five principals may have met to consider the state requirements for being a principal, national school leader standards, local training offerings and any local requirements for serving in the role. During

Degrees and Professional Licensure	25 Points Required	
Activities	Possible	Earned
Bachelor's Degree	5	
Master's Degree	10	
K-12 Principal Licensure	15	
Work Experiences	**25 Points Required**	
Activities	Possible	Earned
Teaching (1 point/year, 5 points minimum)	25	
Curriculum or Instructional Facilitator (5 points/year)	20	
Instructional Coach (5 points/year)	20	
Assistant Principal or Dean of Students (10 points/year)	20	
Central Office Director or Above (10 points/year)	20	
Workshops and Training	**15 Points Required**	
Activities	Possible	Earned
Building a Standards Based Interview Protocol	3	
Creating a Culture for School Success	3	
Data Driven Decision Making	3	
Equity, Diversity and Inclusion	3	
Leading School Improvement Initiatives	3	
MTSS	3	
Partnering with Parents	3	
Providing Effective Feedback	3	
Scheduling for Student Success	3	
Successful Co-Teaching with SPED Specialists	3	
Activities and Experiences	**20 Points Required**	
Activities	Possible	Earned
Job Shadowing of a Master Principal (50+ hours)	5	
Mentor Teacher (50+ hours)	5	
School Leadership Team Member (2+ years)	5	
Develop and Deliver Site-Based Training (10+ hours)	5	
Plan and Lead a Significant School or District Event	5	
Present at a State or National Level Conference	5	
Academies and Certificates	**15 Points Required**	
Activities	Possible	Earned
Aspiring Leaders Academy	15	
Strategic Human Capital Academy	15	
Instructional Coaching Certificate	10	
Teacher Leader Certificate	5	
Academically Gifted Certificate	5	
English as a Second or Other Language Certificate	5	
Total Points Earned		

Figure 11.1 Sample-Guided Pathway for the Role of Principal

the design process, points can be distributed across categories in order to weight different skills, knowledge and aptitudes differently. Meant to be customized by each school or district, the Guided Pathways serve as a transparent approach to communicating to educators what they need to know and be able to do in order to be considered for a job role. Guided Pathways are accessible and tangible, creating trust in the promotion process.

Table 11.3 Action Steps for Promoting

Best Practice	Data/Resources	Lead	Timeline

 # Action Steps for Promoting

With your Talent Development Team, identify next steps in becoming more strategic in your promoting practices.

- Which best practices are you already using to successfully promote educators?
- Which new practices would you like to begin implementing?
- In Table 11.3, list new practices for implementation, data/resources needed, a lead team member and the timeline for putting your next steps into action.

 # Talent Analytics for Promoting

You have now assessed your current practices and identified some action steps. Below are the talent analytics, found in the Strategic Talent Leadership Scorecard (Appendix C), that you can use to measure and track your progress toward being a strategic talent leader.

1. Critical leadership roles by risk rating
2. Number of successors identified for each critical leadership role
3. Employees, by job classification, who report knowing how to seek a promotion
4. Employees, engaged in pre-promotion activities, who are promoted from within
5. Employees, by job classification, who engaged in a career coaching session

Case Study Response

Now that you have learned more about best practices for promoting educators, what advice would you give to Tina Sonricker's superintendent? Write your response in the space below:

_____

_____

_____

_____

_____

References

Andrianova, S., Maor, D., & Schaninger, B. (2018). *Winning with your talent management strategy*. McKinsey & Company. Retrieved from: https://www.mckinsey.com/business-functions/organization/our-insights/Winning-with-your-talent-management-strategy

Burgess, W. (2016). Why companies overlook great internal candidates. *Harvard Business Review*, October 3, 2016. Retrieved from: https://hbr.org/2016/10/why-companies-overlook-great-internal-candidates

Cieminski, A. B. (2018). Practices that support leadership succession and principal retention. *Education Leadership Review, 19*(1), pp. 21–41.

Mercer. (2015). *Career frameworks: The strategic centerpiece of integrated talent management* [white paper]. Retrieved from: https://www.mercer.ca/en/our-thinking/career-frameworks-report.html

Meyer, D. K., & Lenarz, K. (2019). New educators want opportunities for teacher leadership, too. *ASCD Express, 14*(33).

Parfitt, C. M. (2017). Creating a succession-planning instrument for educational leadership. *Education Leadership Review, 18*(1), pp. 21–36.

Peters-Hawkins, A. L., Reed, L. C., & Kingsberry, F. (2018). Dynamic leadership succession: Strengthening urban principal succession planning. *Urban Education, 53*(1), pp. 26–54.

Rothwell, W. J. (2005). *Effective succession planning: Ensuring leadership continuity and building talent from within* (3rd ed.). New York, NY: AMACOM.

Sabina, L. L., & Colwell, C. (2018). Challenges of principal succession-examining the challenges of hiring internal vs. external candidates. *Athens Journal of Education, 5*(4), pp. 375–395.

Smith, S. V. (2012). No career path, no retention. *Forbes Magazine*, November 12, 2012. Retrieved from: https://www.forbes.com/sites/sylviavorhausersmith/2012/11/12/no-career-path-no-retention/#520b738b56dd

Stanier, M. B. (2020). *How knowing this one date will change how you look at work forever* [blog post]. Retrieved from: https://boxofcrayons.com/2017/09/how-knowing-this-one-date-will-change-how-you-look-at-work-forever/

Retaining

Three years ago, Principal Wyche took on the challenge of taking over a turn-around elementary school. Each year, she strategically retained the strongest teachers and coached out the low-performing ones, creating vacancies that she filled with top talent. Under her leadership, the faculty and student culture shifted to one that was more collaborative. This last year, her students achieved high growth for the very first time in the history of the school! The students, parents and faculty participated in a huge celebration at the end of the year to mark the incredible achievement. That summer, Wyche and her leadership team met on their own time to map out a strategy to build upon their momentum and ensure that the school continued to grow and reach their next set of goals. They loved working together as a team—it felt like family! Then the phone rang. The superintendent informed Wyche that she was immediately being transferred to a low-performing middle school that needed her to duplicate the results she attained at the elementary school. Principal Wyche resigned from the district that next week.

Retaining Talent

Retaining is the practice of creating a highly engaged workforce that is motivated to remain working for your organization. Feeling valued by their organization, having meaningful work and understanding the pathway to additional opportunities are consistently cited as the top three reasons employees remain with an organization (Kaye & Jordan-Evans, 2014). Monetary compensation does not show up until the fourth or fifth ranked item on most employee retention surveys. But, it is important to note that all retention is not the same. Smart retention is the practice of retaining your most effective employees while coaching out your ineffective employees, allowing you to increase the overall effectiveness of your faculty. A well-crafted retention strategy will support the development of a highly effective team that then attracts other highly effective talent.

To create an effective retention strategy, leaders must first understand retention patterns and drivers of retention across the United States, their region and within their own school district. Schools in high poverty regions, where a lack of food, clothing and shelter impact students' ability to focus on learning versus survival, find it more difficult to retain the very best educators. It is, therefore, not surprising that Carver-Thomas and Darling-Hammond found that teacher turnover rates in Title I schools are 50 percent higher than in non-Title I schools (2017). The authors identified other significant differences in attrition including that STEM teachers leave Title I schools at a rate 70 percent greater than non-Title I schools and that alternatively certified teachers leave at an 80 percent higher rate from Title I schools. And, schools whose populations are majority minority experience attrition that is 70 percent higher than majority white schools. Our most fragile schools and students are further disadvantaged by the churn of teachers coming in and out of their classrooms, negatively impacting student achievement (Ronfeldt, Loeb, & Wyckoff, 2013), disrupting school improvement momentum, breaking relationships with the community and families and exacerbating a culture of instability. One difference maker seems to be schools that participate in urban teacher residency programs. Papay, West, Fullerton, and Kane (2012) conducted a program evaluation to determine the impact of urban teacher residency programs. One of their findings was that a robust teacher preparation and support model had a significant impact on teacher retention. Compared to urban school districts who retain 50 percent of their teachers after the first three years, urban teacher residency programs were able to retain 90 percent of teachers. For strategic talent leaders of highly impacted schools, this is evidence that the provision of beginning teacher mentoring, training, coaching and support can counterbalance the challenges of poverty on teacher working conditions.

But eventually, pay does matter. Gray and Taie (2015) followed a cohort of beginning teachers through their first five years. After their first year of teaching, 97 percent of teachers with a starting salary of over $40,000 were still teaching compared to only 87 percent of those with salaries less than $40,000. Three years later, the difference was still nine percentage points. Similarly, in the Learning Policy Institute's report of teacher attrition, Carver-Thomas and Darling-Hammond (2017) reported that in Northeast states that offered higher average pay and smaller class sizes, teacher turnover was only 10 percent compared to states in the South which have the highest annual turnover rate at 16 percent. When teacher compensation is high and working conditions are supportive, schools are able to retain highly effective teachers who will remain in the profession and in their schools longer (Loeb, Beteille, & Kalogrides, 2012). Tracking your school and district retention data, measuring working conditions and employing smart retention practices are all strategies that will support you in becoming a strategic talent leader.

Strategic Talent Leadership Insights for Retaining

With your Strategic Talent Leadership Team, review the strategic talent leadership practices for retaining (see Table 12.1). If you are currently engaging in a practice, check 'yes.' If not, check 'not yet' and consider how this practice could be adopted by your organization as you read through the best practices described in this chapter.

Table 12.1 Strategic Talent Leadership Insights for Retaining

Strategic Practice	Yes	Not Yet
Our organization annually surveys employees about working conditions to inform retention strategies.		
Our organization analyzes retention rates by demographic to inform retention strategies.		
Our organization analyzes retention data by educator effectiveness rating to support smart retention practices by school.		
Our organization analyzes annual educator attendance rates by school.		
Our organization uses stay interviews to retain our most effective employees.		

Best Practices for Retaining Talent

Survey Employees about Working Conditions

At some point in your education career, you have likely ended up social-izing with other educators outside of school. Stories fly, tales of student mishaps are shared and bragging rights are cashed in. That is where I learned that not all schools had 'bucket brigades' for leaky roofs on rainy days and that not all teachers had to bring their own toilet paper to work. It is where I learned that some of my peers taught at schools where the Parent Teacher Association (PTA) decorated the faculty lounge and brought baked goods on Fridays. That at some schools, teachers were given cash cards of $1,000 to buy supplies at the beginning of the year. Working con-ditions vary greatly from school to school and depend upon many factors including the engagement level of the PTA, allocation of resources by the principal, funding from the district and county, but, most importantly, stra-tegic efforts on the part of administrators to remove barriers to educator success. While the baked goods and cash cards are nice, they are super-ficial contributors to working conditions. The most impactful aspects of working conditions *can* be controlled regardless of funding because they are tied to human behaviors. In an annual survey of employees across the United States, Cole (2018) reported that 34 percent of workers had not been recognized or thanked for their contributions in over a year. Strategic talent leaders understand the value of employee recognition and its impact on retention. In a retention study of beginning teachers, Aragon (2016) documented the most frequently cited reasons for attrition. They included a lack of recognition, loss of autonomy, limited or nonexistent performance feedback and a lack of advancement opportunities. This led to a five-year cohort attrition rate of 46 percent. However, the companion figure that is often left out of this story is that only 17 percent left teaching altogether. The remaining 29 percent stayed in education but switched schools or districts. This migration from one school to another can be prevented by improving working conditions. The leadership behaviors that control work-ing conditions are not dependent upon funding from the district, the state or even the PTA. They are free. But, in order to improve your working conditions, you must understand how they are perceived by educators. An efficient way to collect this data is through an annual Working Conditions

Survey. North Carolina conducts such a survey statewide every two years (https://ncteachingconditions.org/) and offers robust reporting to the public and schools in an effort to improve working conditions. Their research, questions and resources are available online to anyone. There are also organizations that offer fee-based surveys that can be used at the school or district level. Often, these include additional audiences such as students and parents. Whether you leverage an existing survey or create your own, collecting and analyzing data related to educator perceptions of working conditions can be valuable driver of your retention strategy.

Analyze Retention Data by Demographic

Knowing your school and district retention rate is valuable. But, knowing your retention rate by teacher demographic is strategic. The ability to under-stand *who* you are losing from your organization enables you to be more strategic in your efforts to retain top talent. Nationally, the teacher turn-over rate is 16 percent (Carver-Thomas & Darling-Hammond, 2019). This includes eight percent that leave education and eight percent that migrate, or switch schools. But, not all demographic groups leave at the same rate (Ingersoll & May, 2011). Marvel, Lyter, Peltola, Strizek, and Morton (2007) analyzed subgroup attrition from Schools and Staffing Surveys (SASS) and Teacher Follow-Up Study (TFS) and found that teachers of color left the profession at higher rates than White teachers:

- All teachers of color, 19.4%
- Blacks, 20.7%
- Latinos, 19.4%
- Asians and Pacific Islanders, 18.2%
- Whites, 16.1%

In the United States, 40 percent of students enrolled in public schools are of color but only 17 percent of public school teachers are people of color (Achinstein, Ogawa, Sexton, & Freitas, 2010; Bristol, 2015). Increasing the recruitment and retention of teachers of color is beneficial to all students but especially to students of color who, when taught by teachers of color, demonstrate "improved reading and math test scores, improved graduation rates, and increases in aspirations to attend college" (Carver-Thomas, 2018, p. 1). Knowing the benefits of having a diverse teacher workforce that mirrors our diverse student population makes it even more imperative that we track teacher attrition by demographic and build retention strategies that are responsive to these patterns.

Analyze Smart Retention Practices

If you had the opportunity to swap out your weakest teachers for more effective ones, would you? Most principals would answer with a resounding 'Yes!' And, yet, retention rates of teachers continue to be reported in the aggregate and are not broken down by teacher effectiveness level, allowing principals to more fully understand the talent profile of their school. Retaining one-hundred percent of your highly effective teachers should be the goal of every administrator. But, retaining one-hundred percent of underperforming teachers would only make improving outcomes for students more difficult. The ideal retention pattern is what TNTP (2012) calls 'smart retention.'

Smart retention practices result in increasing the retention rate of high performers while decreasing the retention rate of low performers. Table 12.2 illustrates that the strategic principal retained a decreasing percentage of low-performing teachers over time, replacing those teachers with average and high performers. At the start of the data tracking, 16 percent of the faculty were high performing. After five years, 36 percent were high performing, more than a 100 percent increase. More importantly, the percentage of low-performing teachers decreased from

Table 12.2 Sample Smart Retention Trend for a Faculty of Fifty

Teacher Effectiveness Level	2017–2018	2018–2019	2019–2020	2020–2021	2021–2022
High	8/10 (80%)	10/12 (83%)	12/14 (86%)	16/16 (100%)	18/18 (100%)
Average	25/30 (83%)	25/28 (89%)	26/29 (90%)	27/29 (93%)	26/27 (96%)
Low	10/10 (100%)	7/10 (70%)	5/7 (70%)	2/5 (40%)	0/5 (0%)

20 percent of the faculty to zero. In the 2017–2018 school year, the principal would not have been able to close the achievement gap because she did not have the teacher talent to do so. Now, with 100 percent of her faculty at average or high performance levels, she can achieve high growth and improve outcomes for all students.

In an effort to help principals to retain more high-performing teachers, I worked with a team of master teachers to interview educators who were able to consistently achieve more than a year's worth of growth out of their students. These irreplaceable teachers (TNTP, 2012) take an average of 11 hires to replace (TNTP, 2012). Highly effective minority teachers are even more likely to leave than their white counterparts, making them even more irreplaceable (Pratt, Booker, &Tennessee Department of Education, 2014). During the interviews and focus groups, these irreplaceable teachers told us that what keeps them at their school is that they have autonomy to do what they know is best for students and that their principals give them the flexibility to try new strategies. Whereas other teachers might be required to turn in weekly lesson plans and meet regularly with an instructional coach, these teachers were exempt from the requirements and allowed to 'do their own thing.' This same group of teachers shared that if principals failed to recognize their effectiveness and subjected them to using district-provided lesson plans or scripted curriculum, they would leave. Principals who do not track the effectiveness rates risk losing their most valuable assets in achieving their student achievement goals.

Analyze Educator Attendance Rates

The average national teacher attendance rate is 94 percent, but approximately 16 percent of teachers are chronically absent, missing 18 or more school days. The impact of chronic teacher absences is the difference between having teacher with one to two years of experience versus three to five years (Clotfelter, Ladd, & Vigdor, 2007; Miller, 2008; Miller, Murnane, & Willett, 2008). And, students living in poverty experience teacher absence rates significantly higher than their peers (Clotfelter et al., 2007). Teacher daily attendance *is* a form of teacher retention. And, while many districts closely attend to annual teacher retention, not all consider the daily and annual teacher attendance rates as important. From a strategic talent leadership perspective, having the greatest factor impacting student achievement, teachers, in the classroom every single day is critical to improving student outcomes. In an analysis of a large, urban, district's daily attendance rates, Fridays and the days before or after a holiday were the most frequent days missed by teachers. In order to combat this practice of extending breaks, districts should consider instituting policies preventing teacher absences before or after holidays. Other absence reducing practices to consider include:

- Launching a teacher attendance initiative that recognizes teachers with high or perfect attendance.
- Creating an incentive program that allows teachers to sell back their sick days at the end of each year as a bonus for not taking leave.
- Holding all professional development during the summer, on weekends and on teacher workdays (giving trade time or a stipend to teachers for weekend or summer days).
- Initiating a penalty for missing more than 10 student days (as a last resort).

A strategic teacher retention plan goes beyond examining annual retention rates. It considers the daily attendance of educators and seeks to increase the number of days that students are taught by a certified, qualified teacher.

Work the Grapevine

The proverbial grapevine is your school's underground communication channel. It is where you learn who is seeking a promotion, who might be interviewing for other jobs and who is unhappy with their job, among other information. The grapevine is ripe with gossip and if you are not leveraging it as an informal, unofficial source of data to inform your retention strategy, you are missing out on valuable material. Although it is not advisable to cite grapevine gossip in an exchange with a teacher, it can prompt you to initiate a discovery conversation that may create an entry point for a teacher to reveal his/her plans to leave. Strategic Talent Leadership Tool 12 is a conversation protocol that can be used to facilitate such a conversation. The end goal of any conversation of this type is to better understand the drivers of your school's retention and attrition.

Strategic Talent Leadership Tool 12—The Stay Interview

Principal Wyche's superintendent did not invest time in having a career conversation with her. Had he done so, he would have learned that Wyche had invested 80-hour work weeks for the past three years in order to turn her school around from one that was identified by the state as low-performing to one that achieved high growth. Now that this goal was achieved, she and her team were looking forward to a healthier work-life balance. The hardest work was behind them and they were looking forward to continuing to grow their school using the momentum they had built up for three years. None of them wanted to leave the school. And, Wyche certainly had no desire to begin the process all over again with another school. As a result of not understanding what his star principal valued, he lost her. What could have prevented this loss? A stay interview.

Stay interviews differ from exit interviews in that they are conducted during employment, when decisions to leave have not yet been made. While the purpose of an exit interview is to understand *why* an employee left, the purpose of a stay interview is to know how to prevent an employee from ever leaving. The interview can be a single, targeted conversation or a series of short and ongoing conversations that lead a supervisor to better understand how to support and retain a key team member. And the answer to the question, "How frequently should I conduct stay interviews?" is "As often as needed to retain your top talent!" Strategic Talent Leadership Tool 12 offers suggested stay interview questions (Figure 12.1). Supervisors are encouraged to add their own questions that will help them to best cull out of their team members the information needed in order to provide strong leadership that leads to retention.

With the greatest consistency, each of the stay interviews I ever conducted ended with my team member stating that she/he had never before

Set the Stage
First, welcome your team member and thank them for being willing to meet. Identify a specific contribution that they are making or have made to the organization that you highly value. Transition into the stay interview questions by explaining that you do not want to lose the value that they bring to your school/district/organization and for that reason, you'd like to learn more about them.
Question 1
What do you enjoy most about your current role?
Question 2
Is there anything that I can do to better support you in your role?
Question 3
What other opportunities would you like to have in this school/district/organization?
Question 4
Is there anything that would ever make you decide to leave this organization?
Question 5
Is there anything I haven't asked about that you would like to share with me?
Close the Conversation
Thank your team member for engaging in conversation. Assure him/her that everything you discusses will be kept in confidence. If follow-up steps were identified, explain how you will follow-up and expected next steps.

Figure 12.1 Stay Interview Questions

been asked those types of questions and that they greatly appreciated the opportunity to be listened to. Stay interviews address the very working conditions that surveyed employees report are most important—they want to be valued, they want their work to have meaning and they want to know that there are additional opportunities to be successful in the organization. And, you as a leader now have a blueprint for retaining and growing your top talent.

Table 12.3 Action Steps for Retaining

Best Practice	Required Resources	Lead	Timeline

 ## Action Steps for Retaining

With your Talent Development Team, identify next steps in becoming more strategic in your retention practices.

- Which best practices are you already using to successfully retain top talent?
- Which new practices would you like to begin implementing?
- In Table 12.3, list new practices for implementation, data/resources needed, a lead team member and the timeline for putting your next steps into action.

Talent Analytics for Retaining

You have now assessed your current practices and identified some action steps. Below are the talent analytics, found in the Strategic Talent Leadership Scorecard (Appendix C), that you can use to measure and track your progress towards being a strategic talent leader.

1. Employee responses to annual working conditions surveys
2. Retention data by demographic (experience level, licensure type, race, gender, etc.)
3. Smart Retention practices by school (retention by effectiveness rating)
4. Annual educator attendance rates
5. Stay Interviews conducted by position type

Case Study Response

Now that you have learned more about best practices for retaining educators, what advice would you give to Principal Wyche's superintendent? Write your response in the space below:

_____

_____

_____

_____

_____

References

Achinstein, B., Ogawa, R. T., Sexton, D., & Freitas, C. (2010). Retaining teachers of color: A pressing problem and a potential strategy for "hard-to-staff" schools. *Review of Educational Research*, *80*(1), pp. 71–107. https://www.jstor.org/stable/40658446

Aragon, S. (2016). *Teacher shortages: What we know*. Denver, CO: The Education Commission of the States.

Bristol, T. (2015). *White House Initiative on Educational Excellence for African Americans/Stanford Center for Opportunity Policy in Education (SCOPE) Recruiting & Retaining Teachers of Color Webinar*. https://sites.ed.gov/whieeaa/files/2014/01/Resource-Slides.pdf

Carver-Thomas, D. (2018). *Diversifying the teaching profession: How to recruit and retain teachers of color*. Palo Alto, CA: Learning Policy Institute.

Carver-Thomas, D., & Darling-Hammond, L. (2019). The trouble with teacher turnover: How teacher attrition affects students and schools. *Education Policy Analysis Archives*, *27*(36). http://dx.doi.org/10.14507/epaa.27.3699

Carver-Thomas, D., & Darling-Hammond, L. (2017). *Teacher turnover: Why it matters and what we can do about it*. Palo Alto, CA: Learning Policy Institute.

Clotfelter, C. T., Ladd, H. F., & Vigdor, J. L. (2007). *Are teacher absences worth worrying about in the U.S.?* Cambridge: National Bureau of Economic Research.

Cole, M. (2018). A little goes a long way. *Talent Development*, March, 2018.

Gray, L., & Taie, S. (2015). *Public school teacher attrition and mobility in the first five years: Results from the first through fifth waves of the 2007–08 beginning teacher longitudinal study (NCES 2015-337).* U.S. Department of Education. Washington, DC: National Center for Education Statistics. Retrieved from http://nces.ed.gov/pubsearch.

Ingersoll, R. M., & May, H. (2011). Recruitment, Retention and the Minority Teacher Shortage. *Consortium for Policy Research in Education.* CPRE Research Report #RR-69. Retrieved from: http://repository.upenn.edu/cgi/viewcontent.cgi?article=1232&context=gse_pubs

Kaye, B., & Jordan-Evans, S. (2014). *Love 'em or lose 'em: getting good people to stay.* San Francisco, CA: Berrett-Koehler Publishers.

Loeb, S., Beteille, T., & Kalogrides, D. (2012). Effective schools: Teacher hiring, assignment, development, and retention. *Education Finance and Policy, 7*(3), pp. 269–304.

Marvel, J., Lyter, D. M., Peltola, P., Strizek, G. A., & Morton, B. A. (2007). *Teacher attrition and mobility: Results from the teacher follow-up survey, 2004-05, first look.* Washington, DC: National Center for Educational Statistics.

Miller, R. T., Murnane, R. J., & Willett, J. B. (2008). Do teacher absences impact student achievement? Longitudinal evidence from one urban school district. *Educational Evaluation and Policy Analysis, 30*(2), pp. 181–200.

Miller, R. (2008). *Tales of teacher absence: New research yields patterns that speak to policymakers.* Washington, DC: Center for American Progress.

Papay, J. P., West, M. R., Fullerton, J. B., & Kane, T. J. (2012). Does an urban teacher residency increase student achievement? Early evidence from Boston. *Educational Evaluation and Policy Analysis, 34*(4), pp. 413–434.

Pratt, T. Booker, L., & Tennessee Department of Education. (2014). *Teacher retention in Tennessee: Are we keeping our best teachers? Policy Brief. Tennessee Department of Education.* Tennessee Department of Education.

Ronfeldt, M., Loeb, S., & Wyckoff, J. (2013). How teacher turnover harms student achievement. *American Educational Research Journal, 5*(1), pp. 4–36. Retrieved from: https://cepa.stanford.edu/content/how-teacher-turnover-harms-student-achievement.

TNTP. (2012). *The Irreplaceables: Understanding the real retention crisis in America's urban schools.* New York City, NY: TNTP. https://tntp.org/publications/view/the-irreplaceables-understanding-the-real-retention-crisis

13 | Conclusion

The Exponential Impact

The Strategic Talent Leadership Framework is a system, like a human body, and works best when all components are working *with* each other, in alignment. If you break your foot, for example, the rest of your body still works but, over time, you will develop lower back and hip pain from favoring your good foot. Or, you may have to rely on the external tool of crutches to enable you to walk while your broken foot is healing. Similarly, if some of your strategic talent leadership practices are broken or weak, it will eventually impact other practices and may require you to rely upon external resources. If your weak retention practices are leading to high attrition, it will put stress upon your forecasting, recruiting and hiring practices. You may have to rely upon the 'crutch' of an external recruiting company to help provide you with international teachers, online teachers or long-term substitutes. While these sources of teachers are not necessarily bad, they are not sustainable. They are a temporary tool to help bridge you to a more effective retention strategy. In Table 13.1—Strategic Talent Leadership Drivers— the relationships among all 12 Strategic Talent Leadership functions are described in terms of which functions drive success in other functions. In many cases, functions are reciprocal drivers of each other. Forecasting practices impact, recruiting and hiring practices. You cannot recruit or hire if you do not know what your vacancies are. Therefore, forecasting serves as a driver for these two other functions.

Table 13.1 Strategic Talent Leadership Drivers

➡ = Key Driver / ⇄ = Reciprocal Drivers	Forecasting	Recruiting	Hiring	Assigning	Onboarding	Inducting	Training	Coaching	Evaluating	Compensating	Promoting	Retaining
Forecasting		➡	➡								⇄	⇄
Recruiting			➡	➡							⇄	⇄
Hiring				➡	➡	➡	➡	➡			⇄	⇄
Assigning					➡	➡	➡	➡				➡
Onboarding		➡				➡	➡	➡				➡
Inducting		➡					➡	➡				➡
Training		➡						➡	➡	➡	➡	➡
Coaching		➡							➡	➡	➡	➡
Evaluating										➡	➡	➡
Compensating		➡									➡	➡
Promoting	⇄	⇄	⇄									➡
Retaining	⇄	⇄	⇄									

On the other hand, recruiting and promoting are reciprocal drivers of each other. They impact each other in that if I promote a team member, it recreates a new vacancy for which I have to recruit. Forecasting, recruiting, hiring, promoting and retaining are all reciprocal drivers in this way because they are so tightly aligned within the overall Strategic Talent Leadership system.

It is from the alignment across the talent leadership practices that the Strategic Talent Leadership Framework draws its strength. In support of alignment, this book was designed around 4 domains and 12 functions. Within each function, you are provided five best practices and one tool that illustrates how to implement one of the best practices. In total, the 60 best practices are the source of the 60-item Strategic Talent Leadership Site-Based Assessment and the 60-item Strategic Talent Leadership Scorecard. When all best practices across the 4 domains and 12 functions are being implemented, progress monitored and used to inform future practice, the impact upon improved student outcomes is exponential!

Next Steps

So, how are you going to get from here to exponential? The first step is establishing your Strategic Talent Leadership Team. At a district level, this team could comprise the Chief HR Officer (or your equivalent position), recruiters, hiring managers, principals and teacher representatives. If you are using this book as a toolkit at the school level, your current School Leadership Team could dually serve as your Strategic Talent Leadership Team. Or, you could seek out other representatives from across the faculty including administrators, student support services faculty, teachers, classified personnel and even your human resources team member. Encourage all team members to read this book so that everyone is familiar with the domains and functions that make up the framework, the 12 tools, and the research behind talent leadership. When the team shares this foundational knowledge base, you will be ready to take action.

Step 1—Strategic Talent Leadership Site-Based Assessment

Your first step as a Strategic Talent Leadership (STL) team is to conduct a site-based assessment. This instrument is located in Appendix A. As a team, walk through each of the 60 items which are organized by function. If you are currently engaging in the best practice, check the 'yes' column. If you are not using the best practice or if you do not know what the practice is, check the 'not yet' column. It is okay to have a lot of 'not yet's.' That is the whole purpose of the book—to understand what you could be doing to strengthen your strategic talent leadership practices. Total up your yes's and not yet's by function and in the aggregate. With your team, discuss your current areas of strength and decide which functions could be priorities for you in the future. If you have trouble prioritizing, it is recommended that you begin with Domain 1—Talent Acquisition. If you focus on the quality of the talent that you bring onto your team, all other functions will improve. For example, if you hire a stellar teacher who is achieving 1.5+ years of growth with students each year, you do not necessarily have to provide that teacher with a mentor. She/he might even be able to serve as a mentor, lessening the time and effort you will need to invest in him or her. Ideally, start with selecting three to five priority practices to take on for your next school year.

Step 2—Strategic Talent Leadership Action Planner

Now that you have selected your priorities, use the Strategic Talent Leadership Action Planner to document them. Identify each best practice on a separate line. Next, describe the data and resources that will be needed to implement the practice. For example, if you decide to initiate a teacher attendance incentive program, you will need to collect historical information about teacher attendance in your district or school. That data will inform how you create the incentive program. If the program includes the provision of recognition certificates, you will need to plan on having those as a resource. On the other hand, if the program includes a $500 bonus at the end of the year, the resources you will need to secure are monetary. Once you have recorded the needed resources, name a lead who will be responsible for ensuring that the best practice is implemented and progress monitored. The lead doesn't necessarily have to do all of the work, but they do have to provide the leadership for the best practice. Finally, decide upon your timeline for reaching full implementation.

Step 3—Strategic Talent Leadership Scorecard

Once launched, you definitely want to monitor your progress as you implement best practices. For each item on your Action Planner, you should collect baseline data. Using our previous example of a teacher attendance incentive program, you would identify the teacher attendance rate from the prior year to serve as your baseline. Let's pretend that it is a low 90 percent. As a team, you will want to set a goal for the upcoming school year. Perhaps you decide that you would like to reach 92 percent. Record that target and collect teacher attendance rates each month throughout the year, monitoring your progress. Use the Strategic Talent Leadership Scorecard, record your data each time you collect it. If it falls below your target, lean on your STL team to adjust your strategy as necessary. The scorecard was designed to be generic with the intention that each user will modify it to meet their individual district and school needs. Do not be afraid to add new items to the scorecard or to delete metrics that are not priorities for your organization. Do note that each of the 60 assessment items is measured in the scorecard so if you add new metrics, you may also want to add them to your site-based assessment.

Step 4—Strategic Talent Leadership Toolkit

As you identify best practices and adjust your strategies, your toolkit provides you with 12 resources for changing practice. Each of the 12 tools provides you with step-by-step instructions for implementing one of the five best practices discussed in the chapter. And, each of these tools has been successfully used by educators to improve human capital outcomes that lead to improved outcomes for students. As a team, you can change and adopt these tools to meet your individual needs. Add additional best practices from your own organization and share any tools that you create with other districts and schools. Ultimately, when we share our lessons of experience with others, we all get better.

Step 5—Strategic Talent Leadership Calendar

In an effort to help you stay on track, Appendix E provides you with an annual Strategic Talent Leadership Calendar. This calendar is organized by the fiscal year of most districts and schools in that it starts in July and ends in June. This is also in alignment with the academic school year. At the top of the calendar, best practices that should be engaged in year-round are highlighted. Thereafter, monthly priorities are listed and Strategic Talent Leadership Tools are referenced using the abbreviation (T#) indicating Tool and the tool number for easy reference. Because you will likely focus on a smaller number of best practices when you are starting out, delete any items that may distract you and timeline out only those practices that are priorities for your district or school. This will help you to stay on track throughout the year and you can add items in as you are ready to expand your Action Planner to new strategies.

Using the Strategic Talent Leadership Framework, site-based assessment, action planner, scorecard, toolkit and calendar will yield you results. It will be important to gather your STL team together on an annual basis to review your scorecard, document your impact and celebrate your progress. As you do, communicate your accomplishments and results to others— your superintendent, your supervisor, your faculty and your community. Your work is improving outcomes for all students and that, as educators, is our sole purpose. Strategic talent leadership is a systematic approach that strengthens you as a leader, your faculty as educators and students as our future.

Appendix A
The Strategic Talent Leadership Site-Based Assessment

TALENT ACQUISITION

FORECASTING	YES	NO
1. Our organization requires educators to submit nonbinding Declarations of Intent in December of each school year which allows hiring managers the greatest amount of time to plan for new hires.		
2. Our organization opens up an interschool transfer window in January for transfers that will go into effect the following school year.		
3. Our organization requires educators to initiate the retirement process at least six months in advance of the retirement date.		
4. Our organization tracks annual birth rate data to inform future kindergarten cohort enrollment which drives fluctuations in the number of teacher positions needed.		
5. Our organization tracks historical attrition data to forecast future hiring needs.		
RECRUITING	**YES**	**NO**
6. Our organization currently recruits from multiple candidate sources to ensure a strong pipeline of candidates. (Examples: Universities, Grow Your Own Programs, Teach for America, Alternative Certification, Troops to Teachers, Teacher Cadets)		
7. Our organization uses a pipeline tracker so that principals and hiring managers always have access to current recruiting information.		
8. Our organization uses an employee ambassador program to reward referrals that lead to the hire of a new employee.		

	YES	NO
9. Our organization maintains a list of highly effective employees eligible for a returnship (retirees or employees who left the district in good standing who are eligible for re-employment).		
10. Our organization offers incentives such as early contracts and/or signing bonuses to candidates in hard to staff positions.		
HIRING	**YES**	**NO**
11. Our organization screens and interviews candidates year-round, using standards-based interview protocols, ensuring a diverse talent pool at all times.		
12. Our organization hires 90 percent of candidates for the upcoming school year by the end of the current school year.		
13. Our organization over hires for hard-to-staff positions such as STEM, Special Education and English as a Second or Other Language.		
14. Our organization interviews underrepresented candidates for each vacancy.		
15. Our organization leverages reverse interviews to increase candidate satisfaction with job placement.		
TALENT ACQUISITION SUBTOTAL		**/15**

TALENT ACCELERATION

ASSIGNING	**YES**	**NO**
16. Our organization strives to achieve congruence of demographics between educators and students at each school.		
17. Our organization uses site-based educator talent maps to achieve equitable student access to talent across and within schools.		
18. Our organization ensures that first-year teachers are not assigned more than two course preparations per semester.		
19. Our organization monitors transfers in and out of schools by number of teachers and effectiveness level with particular attention paid to highly impacted schools.		
20. Our organization avoids making surplus placements into highly impacted schools.		
ONBOARDING	**YES**	**NO**
21. Our organization engages employees in pre-boarding experiences.		
22. Our organization offers a 90-day onboarding program to all employees regardless of hire date.		
23. Our organization offers up-boarding experiences to certified and classified employees who are being promoted.		

24. Our organization offers Employee Resource Groups to underrepresented populations.		
25. Our organization issues Quality of Hire surveys to supervisors upon completion of new hire 90-day onboarding programs.		
MENTORING	**YES**	**NO**
26. Our organization prepares and supports a carefully selected group of mentors who have a history of achieving positive student outcomes.		
27. Our organization ensures that all beginning teachers receive 90 minutes of mentor support each week for their first three years.		
28. Our organization ensures that all beginning teachers have opportunities to observe multiple master teachers.		
29. Our organization ensures that all beginning teachers use video recordings of themselves to reflect upon their practice.		
30. Our organization tracks beginning teacher progress using an Essential Skills Mastery checklist.		
TALENT ACCELERATION SUBTOTAL		**/15**

TALENT ADVANCEMENT

TRAINING	**YES**	**NO**
31. Our organization aligns all training to professional educator and evaluation standards.		
32. Our organization evaluates all training for impact on student outcomes.		
33. Our organization offers academies to prepare educators for future roles.		
34. Our organization supports educators in crafting individualized training experiences to achieve targeted goals.		
35. Our organization makes our training available to ancillary educators such as recruits, substitutes, student teachers and retirees.		
COACHING	**YES**	**NO**
36. Our organization assesses coaching needs.		
37. Our organization identifies and trains coaches in a variety of areas such as executive coaching for leaders, instructional coaching for teachers and targeted coaching for job performance.		
38. Our organization facilitates fulfilling educator requests for appropriately trained coaches.		
39. Our organization ensures that all coaches set, track and measure goal achievement in collaboration with educators.		

40. Our organization provides coaches with release time or monetary compensation.		
EVALUATING	**YES**	**NO**
41. Our organization provides regular training to evaluators to ensure consistency in practices.		
42. 42. Our organization conducts cross-tab analyses to identify instances of overestimated and underestimated teacher performance.		
43. Our organization uses teacher evaluation ratings to make strategic student assignments to benefit the most fragile students.		
44. Our organization tracks and analyzes evaluation results by licensure granting college/university.		
45. Our organization uses evaluation results to inform other talent functions such as hiring, training, coaching, promotion and retention.		
TALENT ADVANCEMENT SUBTOTAL		**/15**

TALENT ASSESSMENT

COMPENSATING	**YES**	**NO**
46. Our organization ensures that educator base salaries (without additional incentives) are equitable across Title I and non-Title I schools.		
47. Our organization's educator compensation plan includes monetary and nonmonetary rewards.		
48. Our organization's compensation plan is structured to be responsive to market demands.		
49. Our organization's compensation plan is designed to achieve locally identified talent goals.		
50. Our organization's compensation plan is accurately understood by current and potential employees.		
PROMOTING	**YES**	**NO**
51. Our organization assigns annual risk ratings to all critical leadership positions.		
52. Our organization has three or more potential successors identified for each critical leadership position.		
53. Our organization has clear and communicated processes for seeking promotions.		
54. Our organization uses pre-promotion strategies to upskill employees for future roles.		
55. Our organization offers career coaching opportunities to all employees.		
RETAINING	**YES**	**NO**
56. Our organization annually surveys employees about working conditions to inform retention strategies.		

57. Our organization analyzes retention rates by demographic to inform retention strategies.		
58. Our organization analyzes retention data by educator effectiveness rating to support smart retention practices by school.		
59. Our organization analyzes annual educator attendance rates by school.		
60. Our organization uses stay interviews to retain our most effective employees.		
TALENT ASSESSMENT SUBTOTAL		/15

The Strategic Talent Leaderhip Site-Based Assessment

Results Summary

DOMAIN	SUBTOTAL SCORE
Talent Acquisition	/15
Talent Acceleration	/15
Talent Advancement	/15
Talent Assessment	/15
Total Site-Based Analysis Score	/60

Score Interpretation

0–30   Your organization's talent strategy has many opportunities to grow. Seek out organizations with strong talent strategies and conduct site visits. Establish an organization to organization mentorship with the goal of strengthening your talent strategy. Create a two- to three-year full implementation plan for your Strategic Talent Leadership best practices. Annually assess your progress by repeating this site-based assessment.

31–40   Your organization is working towards a cohesive talent strategy. Prioritize the practices that will best address your critical needs and focus on those for this year. Schedule the implementation of other Strategic Talent Leadership best practices for the following school year. Annually assess your progress by repeating this site-based assessment.

41–50   Your organization has a strong talent strategy. Identify new Strategic Talent Leadership best practices that could further strengthen your talent strategy and bring you to full implementation. Annually assess your progress by repeating this site-based assessment.

51–60   Your organization has a cohesive talent strategy. Capture and share your model practices with other organizations while continuing to strive for full implementation of best practices in each domain and function area.

Appendix B
The Strategic Talent Leadership Action Planner

FORCASTING			
Best Practice	**Data/Resources**	**Lead**	**Timeline**

RECRUITING			
Best Practice	**Data/Resources**	**Lead**	**Timeline**

HIRING			
Best Practice	**Data/Resources**	**Lead**	**Timeline**

ASSIGNING			
Best Practice	**Data/Resources**	**Lead**	**Timeline**

ONBOARDING			
Best Practice	**Data/Resources**	**Lead**	**Timeline**

MENTORING			
Best Practice	**Data/Resources**	**Lead**	**Timeline**

TRAINING			
Best Practice	**Data/Resources**	**Lead**	**Timeline**

COACHING			
Best Practice	**Data/Resources**	**Lead**	**Timeline**

EVALUATING			
Best Practice	**Data/Resources**	**Lead**	**Timeline**

COMPENSATING			
Best Practice	**Data/Resources**	**Lead**	**Timeline**

PROMOTING			
Best Practice	**Data/Resources**	**Lead**	**Timeline**

RETAINING			
Best Practice	**Data/Resources**	**Lead**	**Timeline**

Appendix C
The Strategic Talent Leadership Scorecard

This scorecard is provided as a sample. It is recommended that each user customize it to fit their needs by adding/subtracting rows and modifying content such that it aligns to the specific makeup of their school or district.

	2020–2021		2021–2022		2022–2023	
FORECASTING	#	%	#	%	#	%
1. Educators who indicated on their Declaration of Intent that they intend to:						
Remain						
Transfer						
Take a Leave of Absence						
Retire						
2. Educators who secured an interschool transfer by school:						
School A						
School B						
School C (add rows as needed)						
3. Educators eligible for retirement by position:						
Administrators						
Teachers						
Classified						

4. Positions to be added or subtracted based upon changes in enrollment:						
K						
1						
2 (add rows as needed)						
5. Positions to be added or subtracted based upon historical attrition patterns:						
K						
1						
2 (add rows as needed)						

	2020–2021		2021–2022		2022–2023	
RECRUITNG	#	%	#	%	#	%
6. Candidates available for hire from diverse sources:						
University A						
University B						
Other School Districts						
Grow Your Own Program						
Alternative Certification (add rows as needed)						
7. Applicant engagement:						
Applicants						
Dropped Out of Application Process						
Screened						
Not Hired						
Hired						
Declined Offer of Hire						
8. Employee Ambassador referrals hired by level or subject area:						
Elementary						
Math						
Science (add rows as needed)						

9. Employees eligible for returnships by licensure area:						
Math						
Science						
Principalship (add rows as needed)						
10. Incentives provided to educators in hard-to-staff positions:						
Early Contracts						
Signing Bonuses						

	2020–2021		2021–2022		2022–2023	
HIRING	#	%	#	%	#	%
11. Standards-Based Interviews conducted per month:						
Elementary						
Math						
Science (add rows as needed)						
12. Teachers hired before the end of the school year:						
Elementary						
Math						
Science (add rows as needed)						
13. Vacancies remaining on the first day of school:						
Elementary						
Math						
Science (add rows as needed)						
14. Candidates of color who pass the screening process compared to Caucasian candidates:						
Administrative Candidates—of Color						
Administrative Candidates—Caucasian						
Teacher Candidates—of Color						
Teacher Candidates—Caucasian						

15. Acceptance rate of job offers:						
Administrators						
Teachers						

ASSIGNING	2020–2021		2021–2022		2022–2023	
	#	%	#	%	#	%
16. Congruence of demographic diversity between educators and students:						
Administrators of Color						
Teachers of Color						
Students of Color						
17. Low-performing teachers by school:						
School A						
School B						
School C (add rows as needed)						
18. Beginning teachers assigned more than two course preparations (elementary teachers excepted).						
School A						
School B						
School C (add rows as needed)						
19. Transfers out of schools by number and effectiveness level:						
School A Transfers Out						
School A Highly Effective Transfers Out						
School B Transfers Out						
School B Highly Effective Transfers Out						
School A Transfers Out (add rows as needed)						
20. Surplus educator placements by school:						
School A						
School B						
School C (add rows as needed)						

	2020–2021		2021–2022		2022–2023	
ONBOARDING	#	%	#	%	#	%
21. New hires who are engaged in pre-boarding experiences before their start date:						
Administrators						
Educators						
Classified						
22. New hires who completed the onboarding process within 90 days of their start date:						
Administrators						
Educators						
Classified						
23. Promoted employees who were provided an up-boarding experience:						
Certified						
Classified						
24. Employees engaged in an Employee Resource Group (ERG):						
African American ERG						
Latinx ERG						
LGBTQ ERG (add rows as needed)						
25. Quality of hire surveys indicating satisfaction with candidate hired by position:						
Administrator						
Teacher						
Classified						

	2020–2021		2021–2022		2022–2023	
MENTORING	#	%	#	%	#	%
26. Mentors are trained to support mentees:						
Mentors with 30+ hours of training						
Mentors with 5+ years of experience re-trained						

27. Beginning teachers receive 90 minutes of mentoring each week for three years:						
1st year mentees receiving 90 minutes per week						
2nd year mentees receiving 90 minutes per week						
3rd year mentees receiving 90 minutes per week						
28. Mentees observe multiple master teachers:						
0 observations						
1–2 observations						
3+ observations						
29. Mentees video their teaching and reflect with their mentors:						
0 recordings and reflections						
1–2 recordings and reflections						
3+ recordings and reflections						
30. Mentors use an Essential Skills Mastery checklist to monitor mentee progress:						
Mentees who mastered >90% of skills						
Mentees who mastered >80% of skills						
Mentees who mastered <80% of skills						

	2020–2021		2021–2022		2022–2023	
TRAINING	#	%	#	%	#	%
31. Training is aligned to professional educator and evaluation standards:						
District-Developed Training						
District-Offered Training, Externally Developed						
External Training						

32. Training is evaluated for impact:						
Level 1—Participant Satisfaction						
Level 2—Knowledge Retention						
Level 3—Job Application						
Level 4—Measurable Impact						
Return on Investment (ROI)						
33. Academies are offered to prepare educators for future roles:						
Student Teachers						
Teacher Leaders						
Aspiring Leaders						
34. Training wheels are used to craft individualized learning experiences to support educators in achieving targeted goals:						
Administrator Training Wheels Completed						
Teacher Training Wheels Completed						
Classified Training Wheels Completed						
35. Trainings are available to ancillary educators:						
Recruit Participation						
Substitute Participation						
Student Teacher Participation						
Retiree Participation (as rows as needed)						

	2020–2021		2021–2022		2022–2023	
COACHING	#	%	#	%	#	%
36. Coaching needs:						
Behavior Management						
Math Content Knowledge						
English as a Second or Other Language (add rows as necessary)						

37. Coaches trained in a variety of areas:						
Executive Coaching						
Instructional Coaching						
Job Performance (add rows as needed)						
38. District-facilitated coaching matches:						
Coaching Requests						
Coaching Matches						
39. Coaching impact:						
Coaching Cycles						
Goals Set						
Goals Achieved						
40. Coaches compensated:						
Partial Release Time Coaches						
Full-Time Release Coaches						
Monetarily Compensated Coaches						

	2020–2021		2021–2022		2022–2023	
EVALUATING	#	%	#	%	#	%
41. Educators rated as ineffective, by school:						
School A						
School B						
School C (add rows as needed)						
42. Alignment of evaluations to student outcomes:						
Educator Effectiveness—Overrated						
Educator Effectiveness—Underrated						
Educator Effectiveness—Aligned						
43. Students at-risk assigned to educators by performance level:						
Assigned to Underperforming Educators						
Assigned to High-Performing Educators						

44. High performing teachers by degree or licensure granting college/university:						
University A						
University B						
University C (add rows as needed)						
45. Evaluation results inform strategic talent leadership functions:						
Underperforming Educators Retained						
High-Performing Educators Retained						
Underperforming Educators Promoted						
High-Performing Educators Promoted						
Underperforming Educators Terminated						
High-Performing Educators Terminated						

	2020–2021		2021–2022		2022–2023	
COMPENSATING	#	%	#	%	#	%
46. Average salary by school type:						
Title I						
Non-Title I						
47. Average salary by educator effectiveness level (defined locally):						
Ineffective						
Effective						
Highly Effective						
48. Average salary by staffing difficulty (defined locally):						
Hard-to-Staff						
Average-to-Staff						
Easy-to-Staff						

49. Educators, by school, qualifying for additional incentives (defined locally):						
School A						
School B						
School C (add rows as needed)						
50. Number and percentage of current and potential employees surveyed who accurately understand the compensation model:						
Current Teachers						
Potential Teachers						
Current Principals						

	2020–2021		2021–2022		2022–2023	
PROMOTING	#	%	#	%	#	%
51. Critical leadership positions by risk rating:						
High						
Medium						
Low						
52. Identified successors for each critical leadership position:						
Chief Academic Officer						
Chief Human Resources Officer						
Chief Finance Officer (add rows as needed)						
53. Employees, by job classification, that reported knowing how to seek a promotion:						
Classified						
Certified						
Administrative						
54. Employees engaged in pre-promotion activities that were promoted from within:						
Classified						
Certified						
Administrative						

55. Employees, by job classification, who engaged in a career coaching session:						
Classified						
Certified						
Administrative						

	2020–2021		2021–2022		2022–2023	
RETAINING	#	%	#	%	#	%
56. Working conditions survey results by item (defined locally):						
Employees Satisfied or Highly Satisfied						
Employees Unsatisfied or Highly Unsatisfied						
Employees Intending Upon Returning						
Employees Intending Upon Leaving						
57. Retention rates by demographic (defined locally):						
Years of Experience (1–3)						
Years of Experience (4–9)						
Years of Experience (10+)						
Asian						
African American						
Caucasian						
Latinx (add rows as needed)						
58. School retention rates by educator effectiveness rating (smart retention):						
School A—Highly Effective Educators						
School A—Ineffective Educators						
School B—Highly Effective Educators						
School B—Ineffective Educators						

59. Annual teacher attendance rates (daily retention) by school:						
School A						
School B						
School C (add rows as needed)						
60. Stay Interviews by job classification:						
Classified						
Certified						
Administrator						

Appendix D
Strategic Talent Leadership Toolkit

Strategic Talent Leadership Tool 1—Declaration of Intent

Strategic Talent Leadership Tool 2—Recruitment Pipeline Tracker

Strategic Talent Leadership Tool 3—Standards-Based Interview Protocol

Strategic Talent Leadership Tool 4—Site-Based Talent Map

Strategic Talent Leadership Tool 5—90-Day Onboarding Playbook

Strategic Talent Leadership Tool 6—Essential Skills Mastery Checklist

Strategic Talent Leadership Tool 7—Training Wheels

Strategic Talent Leadership Tool 8—Capture the Learning

Strategic Talent Leadership Tool 9—Nine-Box Talent Review

Strategic Talent Leadership Tool 10—Differentiated Compensation Planner

Strategic Talent Leadership Tool 11—Guided Pathways

Strategic Talent Leadership Tool 12—The Stay Interview

Strategic Talent Leadership Tool 1— Declaration of Intent

Declaration of Intent

Thank you for considering your career opportunities for the upcoming school year. While it is our goal to retain 100% of our team, we understand that, at times, faculty may leave a school for a promotion, family transfer, leave of absence or other reason. By sharing your nonbinding declaration of intent, you are supporting us in forecasting our future staffing needs and recruiting top educators to join our team. Your response will be held in confidence by the administrative team and will be used only for planning purposes. Should you request a follow-up meeting, please indicate so by checking the box at the bottom of this letter. Thank you for your commitment to our students!

Name: _____

Next school year, I intend to:

☐   Remain at School X in my current position

☐   Remain at School X, but would like to be considered for another position within the school

☐   Transfer to another school or department within the district

☐   Take a leave of absence (FMLA, maternity, disability, etc.)

☐   Retire

☐   Resign to work in another school district

☐   Resign and leave the field of education

Would you like to schedule a follow-up meeting to discuss your future plans with a member of our administrative team?

☐   Yes   ☐   No

Thank you for your response!

Strategic Talent Leadership Tool 2—Recruiting Pipeline Tracker

Position	School	Applicants	Eligible	Interviewed	Recommended for Hire	Offer Made	Offer Accepted	Offer Rejected

Strategic Talent Leadership Tool 3—Standards-Based Interview Protocol

	Standard	Standard	Standard	Standard
Evidence Indicators				
Performance Indicators				
Response Indicators				

Strategic Talent Leadership Tool 4—Site-Based Talent Map

Position	Skill or Knowledge	Skill or Knowledge	Skill or Knowledge	Skill or Knowledge	Skill or Knowledge	Skill or Knowledge

Strategic Talent Leadership Tool 5—90-Day Onboarding Playbook

90-Day Site-Based Onboarding Plan			
Instructions: Each employee should be provided a 90-day site-based onboarding. This form should be used to track completion of onboarding activities. After each time segment, both the supervisor and new employee should initial to signify completion of all activities.			
Employee			
Job Role			
Location			
Principal			
Start Date			
90th Day			
Timeline	**Content/Activity**	**Principal Initials**	**Employee Initials**
First Day			
First Week			
Second Week			

90-Day Onboarding Playbook (Continued)

First Month			
Second Month			
Third Month			
90th Day	90-Day On-Site Onboarding Review		
	Monthly check-in with principal or designee to continue the entire first year		

At the end of the 90-day onboarding period, this completed form should be sent to your school's HR partner for inclusion in the new employee's file.

Strategic Talent Leadership Tool 6—Essential Skills Mastery Checklist

ESSENTIAL SKILLS MASTERY CHECKLIST

For each identified skill, document the date when you:

- Observed a master teacher or mentor modeling the skill (MT)
- Used video to reflect upon your implemented practice of the skill (VR)
- Effectively implemented the skill on two separate occasions (1) (2)

Skill	*MT*	*VR*	*1*	*2*
1.				
2.				
3.				
4.				
5.				
6.				
7.				
8.				
9.				
10.				

Strategic Talent Leadership Tool 7—Training Wheels

Training Wheel for_____

1. What is your learning outcome for this training wheel?

2. What training strategies will you employ to achieve this outcome?

3. Using the Training Wheel below, indicate what percentage of your time and effort will be dedicated to each training strategy.

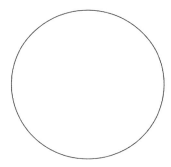

4. How will you evaluate the impact of your learning?

5. How many Continuing Education Units you are seeking?

Name and Date: _____

Strategic Talent Leadership Tool 8—Capture the Learning

Capture the Learning	
Teacher	
Coach	
Date and Time of Session:	
Targeted Goal	
Alignment to Standards	**Professional Teaching Standards**
Coaching Cycle	
Strategy Selected	
Strategy Practice	☐ Observed in a master teacher's classroom ☐ Modeled by coach ☐ Co-taught with coach ☐ Video-taped practice and viewed with coach ☐ Use of a checklist ☐ Other: _____
Results	☐ Goal Met ☐ Goal Not Yet Met
Next Steps	

Strategic Talent Leadership Tool 9—Nine-Box Talent Review

	Weak	Solid	Strong
Move Upward to Meet Potential	**4** Underperformer Document and Develop	**2** Emerging Leader Stretch and Develop	**1** Irreplaceable Stretch and Develop
Move Laterally or Up One Level	**7** Underperformer Document and Develop	**5** Core Talent Develop	**3** Emerging Leader Stretch and Develop
Keep in Current Role Only	**9** Weak Performer Document and Exit	**8** Core Talent Develop	**6** Core Talent Develop

Future Performance Potential

Current Performance Level

225

Strategic Talent Tool 10—Differentiated Compensation Planner

		High Cost Low Impact	High Cost High Impact
Cost	+		
	−	Low Cost Low Impact	Low Cost High Impact
		−	+
		Impact	

Compensation Type	Cost per Person	Audience	Targeted Outcome

Strategic Talent Leadership Tool 11— Guided Pathways

Degrees and Professional Licensure	25 Points Required	
Activities	**Possible**	**Earned**

Work Experiences	25 Points Required	
Activities	**Possible**	**Earned**

Workshops and Training	15 Points Required	
Activities	**Possible**	**Earned**

Activities and Experiences	20 Points Required	
Activities	**Possible**	**Earned**

Academies and Certificates	15 Points Required	
Activities	**Possible**	**Earned**
Total Points Earned		

Strategic Talent Leadership Tool 12— The Stay Interview

Set the Stage

First, welcome your team member and thank them for being willing to meet. Identify a specific contribution that they are making or have made to the organization that you highly value. Transition into the stay interview questions by explaining that you do not want to lose the value that they bring to your school/district/organization and for that reason, you'd like to learn more about them.

Question 1

What do you enjoy most about your current role?

Question 2

Is there anything that I can do to better support you in your role?

Question 3

What other opportunities would you like to have in this school/district/ organization?

Question 4

Is there anything that would ever make you decide to leave this organization?

Question 5

Is there anything I haven't asked about that you would like to share with me?

Close the Conversation

Thank your team member for engaging in conversation. Assure him/her that everything you discuss will be kept in confidence. If follow-up steps were identified, explain how you will follow up and expected next steps.